MAKING AMENDS: JUSTICE FOR VICTIMS AND OFFENDERS

...... But in these cases
We still have judgement here; that we but teach
bloody instructions, which, being taught, return,
To plague the inventor; this even-handed justice
commands the ingredients of our poisoned
chalice to our own lips.

Macbeth

Making Amends: Justice for Victims and Offenders

An evaluation of the SACRO reparation and mediation project

SUE WARNER
Social Work Research Centre
University of Stirling

Avebury
Aldershot · Brookfield USA · Hong Kong · Singapore · Sydney

Published by
Avebury
Ashgate Publishing Limited
Gower House
Croft Road
Aldershot
Hants GU11 3HR
England

Ashgate Publishing Company
Old Post Road
Brookfield
Vermont 05036
USA

A CIP catalogue record for this book is available from the British Library and the US Library of Congress.

ISBN 1 85628 407 7

Printed and Bound in Great Britain by
Athenaeum Press Ltd, Newcastle upon Tyne.

Contents

Series Editor's Preface

Evaluative Studies in Social Work brings together research which has explored the impact of social work services in a variety of contexts and from several perspectives. The vision of social work in this series is a broad one. It encompasses services in residential, fieldwork and community settings undertaken by workers with backgrounds in health and welfare. The volumes will therefore include studies of social work with families and children, with elderly people, people with mental and other health problems and with offenders.

This approach to social work is consistent with contemporary legislation in many countries, including Britain, in which social work has a key role in the assessment of need and in the delivery of personal social services, in health care and in criminal justice. It also continues a long tradition which perceives an integral relationship between social work, social research and social policy. Those who provide social work services are acquainted with the complexities of human need and with the achievements and shortcomings of major instruments of social policy. This knowledge was exploited by, amongst others, Booth, Rowntree and the Webbs in their studies of poverty. Politicians and sociologists have also recognised that, together with the people they try to help, social workers can provide a commentary on the human meaning of public policies and the social issues that grow from private troubles.

This knowledge and experience of the recipients and practitioners of social work is not, of course, immediately accessible to the wider community. A major purpose of research is to gather, organise and interpret this information and, in the studies in this series, to evaluate the impact of social work. Here there are many legitimate interests to consider. First and foremost are direct service users and those who care for them. These are the people who should be the main beneficiaries of social work services. Also to be considered are the personnel of other services for whom liaison and collaboration with social work is essential to their own successful functioning. The needs and views of these different groups may well conflict and it is the researcher's task to identify those tensions and describe social work's response to them.

The problems which confront social work are often extremely complex. They may need to be tackled in a variety of ways; for example, through practical assistance, advocacy, counselling and supervision. Outcomes may be similarly varied and studies of the effectiveness of social work must demonstrate the different kinds of impact it can have. These may entail changes in users' circumstances, behaviour or well being. On these changes, and on the kind of help they have received, users' perspectives must be of great significance. Also of central interest to those who provide or manage services is an understanding of their form and content and the relationship between the problems identified and the statutory responsibilities of social workers and the help given. Social work researchers must therefore take care to study what is actually delivered through social work and how, as well as its outcomes, aspirations and objectives. For good and ill social work has an impact on a large and increasing number of citizens. A major aim of *Evaluative Studies in Social Work* is to increase well informed understanding of social work, based on knowledge about its real rather than imagined activities and outcomes.

The identification of effectiveness, in its various forms, can also not be the end of the story. The costs of the associated services must be studied, set in the context of their effectiveness, to allow the most efficient use of resources.

These demands present major challenges to researchers who have to use, adapt and develop a wide range of research methods and designs. Ingenuity and persistence are both required if evaluative research in social work is to be pursued in contexts often regarded as beyond the scope of such enquiry. *Evaluative Studies in Social Work* intends to make widely available not only the research findings about the impact of social work but also to demonstrate and discuss possible approaches and methods in this important and developing field of enquiry.

The first volumes in this series describe studies undertaken in the Social Work Research Centre at the University of Stirling. The Centre is funded by the Economic and Social Research Council and the Scottish Office to evaluate the effectiveness of social work services. Later volumes may include work carried out elsewhere.

In *Making Amends* Sue Warner describes a detailed study of an innovative reparation and mediation project involving offenders, victims and prosecutors. Reparation and mediation has been suggested as an antidote for many of the problems of Western criminal justice systems. The processes of reparation and mediation have been described as natural approaches to dispute resolution including those involving crimes. In the present climate there is an increased emphasis on the interests of victims, the need to make offenders accountable for their actions and pressures to reduce the use of formal proceedings and of custody. Reparation and mediation projects have been introduced as a means of reconciling these potentially conflicting concerns.

Within the criminal justice system reparation and mediation involves the intervention of a third party who attempts to help the victim and accused find ways for the accused to make amends for the offence which both feel are fair and just. This process can be used at various points as an alternative to formal proceedings or sanctions, or complementarily. For example reparation and mediation has been developed as an alternative course to formal charges and prosecution. Reparation and mediation may also be used as part of prison social work.

The first Scottish reparation and mediation project was established in 1987 by the Scottish Association for the Care and Resettlement of Offenders (SACRO). This was a three-year pilot project introduced with the aims of providing a service for victims; offering a challenging and constructive response for accused; and exploring the potential for using reparation and mediation as an alternative to court proceedings for minor crimes.

During 1990-91 the Social Work Research Centre at Stirling University undertook an evaluation of this project in its two schemes in Edinburgh and Glasgow. The Centre was awarded a grant for this research by the Central Research Unit of the Scottish Home and Health Department. The purpose of this twelve-month study was to evaluate the operation and impact of the schemes from a variety of perspectives and to take account of the schemes' contrasting organisation. One scheme used volunteers and the other paid mediators. Interviews were conducted with procurators fiscal, mediators, victims and accused. Characteristics, progress and outcome were monitored for referrals to the project; there was also a small comparison group of cases in Glasgow for whom data on progress and outcome were collected.

The costs of criminal justice processes and proceedings are increasingly important. A study of the costs of the reparation and mediation projects compared to those of prosecution was therefore carried out by the Personal Social Services Research Unit at Kent University. The two components of the research were closely integrated so that the costs of the schemes could be analysed in the context of their effectiveness.

Taken as a whole the research which this book reports provides a detailed account of the scope and impact of these pioneer schemes. These are discussed in the context of the legal and social policy questions they raise and of national and international developments in reparation and mediation. The hope is that the thorough evaluation of the experience of these Scottish schemes will be a useful reference point for the many people who plan, manage or work in the growing number of reparation and mediation projects in the criminal justice system.

Juliet Cheetham

Acknowledgements

This study would not have been possible without the help, assistance and support of a number of people and agencies. Warm thanks are due to the victims, accused, mediators and staff involved in the SACRO reparation and mediation schemes, particularly Vi Robertson, Phil Walker, Bronwen Currie and Margaret Kelly who coped admirably with the demands of being the subject of a year long evaluation. Previous staff members, Robert Mackay and John O'Neill also contributed a great deal and Robert Mackay continued to provide information and ideas since his departure from SACRO. Thanks are also due to John Phillips for providing details in the costs of the project.

Staff in associated agencies also gave considerable help to the research. These include Graham Ewing, Pete Lawrence, John MacFarlane, Jim Napier and Tom Tumulty. The procurators fiscal in Glasgow and Edinburgh gave generously of their time throughout the research period and special thanks are due to the senior depute fiscals in Edinburgh and past and present assistant procurators fiscal in Glasgow.

The research was funded by the Scottish Home and Health Department and supported by the Central Research Unit. The help, encouragement and advice from Linda Nicholson and Joe Curran were very much welcomed.

Last, but not least, I owe a big thank you to colleagues in the Social Work Research Centre. The grantholders, Juliet Cheetham and Gill

McIvor have contributed a great deal and special thanks are due to Juliet for editing the final version. Pam Lavery, June Watson and Deanna Jamieson have coped magnificently with the various drafts and amendments with patience and humour.

Glossary of terms

Alternative to Prosecution	An optional course of action open to fiscals in cases in which there is sufficient evidence to prosecute where action is required but prosecution is not essential.
Breach	Where a case is terminated due to the breakdown of the agreement made by the accused and referred back to the fiscal.
Corporate Victim	The victim concerned is an organisation rather than a private individual. Includes large or small businesses and statutory and voluntary organisations.
Deferred Prosecution	The fiscal postpones the decision regarding prosecution until satisfied that the accused has undertaken a certain course of action.

Direct Mediation	Involves the victim and accused meeting face-to-face in the presence of a trained mediator. This excludes meetings which have not been prepared for.
Direct Reparation	Where the accused undertakes work directly for the victim; might include repairing damage caused.
Diversion Scheme	The term used to describe a scheme set up to take cases which would otherwise have been prosecuted. Usually operate outwith the fiscal service. Include the Douglas Inch Clinic, Social Work Diversion and reparation and mediation.
Individual Victim	The victim in the case is a private citizen.
Indirect Mediation	Also described as 'shuttle negotiation' where the victim and accused communicate through the mediator, not directly.
Indirect Reparation	Where the accused does not make reparation directly to the victim but to some other person or organisation, usually determined by the victim.
Marking	Process whereby the fiscal decides whether or not to prosecute a case, and if so, in which court and on what charges to proceed. The fiscal writes this decision on the case papers.
Mediation	Process by which a trained mediator helps victims and accused to reach an agreement which will make good the offence. Can be direct or indirect.

No Proceedings	Where the fiscal decides that the case will not be prosecuted in court. This might occur at the point of marking or be deferred until the accused has taken some course of action sanctioned by the fiscal.
Primary Diversion	Where diversion occurs before court proceedings have been initiated.
Reparation	The making of amends by the accused to the victim to compensate for the offence in some way. Might include financial compensation, an apology, a behavioural undertaking or a donation to charity by the accused.
SACRO	Scottish Association for the Care and Resettlement of Offenders, within which the reparation and mediation project is situated.
Time-barring	Certain statutory offences must be prosecuted within six months of the offence or the case be dropped (Criminal Justice (Scotland) Act 1975, Section 331).

1 Introduction

Introduction

Reparation:	'The act or process of making amends.'
Mediation:	'The act of intervening between two parties in order to bring about an agreement.'

Collins English Dictionary

In reparation and mediation a third party intervenes in a dispute to help determine how the situation can best be resolved. Conflict can take many forms, but this study focuses on that occurring between the victims of crime and those accused of offences. Conflict resolution can occur in various ways and forms, ranging from the informal intervention of a friend or family member to the development of formal reparation and mediation schemes, such as those operating in and around the criminal justice systems across Europe, Australasia and the United States. Making amends might include paying financial compensation, apologising or behavioural contracts between the parties.

The history and development of reparation and mediation in the area of criminal justice are well documented (see for example Mackay, 1986; 1989). Over the last ten years there has been considerable expansion of such schemes in the United Kingdom, largely as diversions from court processes and as sanctions. Various reparation and mediation projects operate to divert cases from prosecution (primary diversion) or, at the other extreme, to divert offenders from custody (tertiary diversion). Some projects are run by probation services and others are multi-agency, involving police and social workers in work with juvenile offenders. Some reparation and mediation projects offer dispute resolution facilities to the wider community.

The notion that an offender should make amends to the victim for her or his actions has widespread appeal. The British Crime Surveys and other opinion polls (cited in Wright, 1989) suggest there is support from the general public for reparation and mediation and that a minority would also welcome it as an alternative response to court proceedings. Research into the experiences of victims of crime also suggests there is support for reparation and mediation (Maguire and Corbett, 1987). Some writers have also pointed to the widespread use of reparation and mediation as 'natural' and superior forms of dispute resolution. Nils Christie (1977) has discussed handing back the conflict between victims and offenders to the individuals concerned in preference to what he claims is currently the case, namely that participants become spectators or actors in a dispute which becomes 'owned' by the State (see also Zehr, 1989). Restorative justice is based on the offender making reparation to the victim concerned rather than on inflicting further harm on the offender (Wright, 1992). Reparation and mediation can therefore bring victims and offenders together to find their own resolutions and to close the incident. Some argue this is 'natural justice', the natural way humankind has resolved disputes (Matthews 1989).

In the United Kingdom the rights and needs of victims have been voiced largely through the growing victim support scheme movement and recent Government policy has reflected these concerns. The White Paper, *Crime, Justice and Protecting the Public* (HMSO, 1990) recognises that offenders should be made accountable for their crimes and proposes that greater attention be paid to increasing the compensation made to victims. Another recent policy document, *The Victim's Charter* (HMSO, 1990), acknowledges wide public support for the concept of reparation. The right of the victim to be compensated and the obligation of the accused to make amends are both stressed and seen as having a contribution to make in reducing offending behaviour and easing the burdens on courts and custodial establishments.

There has also been formal support for reparation and mediation in the United Kingdom. In 1984, the Parliamentary All-Party Penal Affairs Group produced a report on compensation of victims and the wider potential of reparation (PAPPAG 1984). The group advocated a number of experimental schemes operating at different points in and around the criminal justice system. Reparation was considered beneficial, acceptable to victims and successful in terms of getting and fulfilling agreements; also it could be achieved without increasing the crime rate or recidivism.

Several authors have documented the development of reparation and mediation in Britain, for example Marshall and Merry (1990) and Mackay (1986). In brief, the first British reparation and mediation scheme, established in Exeter in 1979, aimed at diverting young offenders from prosecution. Almost three years later schemes became available to divert adults from prosecution, in England through the Kettering scheme and in 1987, in Scotland, through the SACRO project. In 1985 the Home Office funded four pilot reparation and mediation schemes. These and a further four independent schemes were researched in considerable detail (Marshall and Merry, 1990). Marshall (1992) has suggested that an important aspect of the appeal of reparation and mediation schemes lay in their potential to meet several aims. First, they provide the chance to compensate victims. Second they seek to make offenders personally accountable for their actions. Third, schemes offer the possibility of reducing recidivism. Fourth they can be used to divert cases from formal procedures and sanctions, thus reducing costs and the burden on courts and prisons.

Marshall and Merry (1990) found that 60 per cent of victims and almost all offenders approached by the projects had agreed to participate, and in 40 per cent of these cases victims and offenders had met face-to-face. Studies from around the world show that acceptance and satisfaction rates are high. Victims and offenders find reparation and mediation a rewarding experience, especially where they meet together. Examples of schemes studied include those in New Zealand (Galaway 1992); in Norway (Gronfors, 1992); in the United States (Umbreit, 1992) and in Germany (Hartmann, 1992). Most schemes operate with less serious offences and offenders and most are located close to the criminal justice system and are linked to formal proceedings and sanctions. Work by Umbreit in the United States illustrates that the approach can also be successfully applied in serious cases (Umbreit, 1989b). The research consistently highlights the benefits of reparation and mediation. Victims appreciate the opportunity to obtain compensation, either material or symbolic, such as an apology; to express their experiences to the offender and to be involved in a constructive response to offending. Offenders face a difficult situation if they have to meet their victims and, if meetings are carefully mediated, can come to appreciate the consequences of their action (Messmer, 1992). Offenders also have a chance to make amends and close the incident without unnecessary stigma. If the schemes operate as diversions the offender can avoid or minimize formal sanctions and procedures. Some studies have suggested that mediation and reparation are particularly effective where the parties are able to meet face-to-face and have even suggested this can reduce the likelihood of reoffending, at least amongst juveniles (Marshall, 1992; Umbreit, 1992)

There is, therefore, a growing body of evidence that reparation and mediation can be used successfully in the resolution of criminal disputes. However, there have been a number of problems identified across schemes. Most of these relate to the location of programmes in close proximity to the criminal justice system. Many schemes have been established by criminal justice agencies, including the police and probation services, and have included amongst their aims the reduction of prosecution or use of custody. Writers have claimed that such proximity leads to ambiguous goals and the loss of the voluntary nature of participation; and both can cause problems for the operation of schemes (Marshall, 1992; Wright, 1992; Gronfors, 1992; Davis, 1989).

Diversion schemes, including those which use reparation and mediation, have been criticised along several dimensions. First, they are said to extend the range of state control into the lives of private individuals (Matthews, 1988; Merry, 1989; Smith et al, 1989a and Smith and Blagg, 1989). This phenomenon is termed 'net widening'. In primary diversion, that is diversion of cases from court proceedings, net widening would have the effect of drawing into the criminal justice system cases which otherwise would not have been prosecuted, to the disadvantage of the accused and the criminal justice system.

Second, there are potential disadvantages in dealing with cases outwith the courts. In a review of the arguments for and against diversion, Matthews (1988) cites research which shows that reparation and mediation used as a diversion can operate to remove crimes related to poor, black or women victims from the rights and safeguards afforded by court proceedings. This not only offers 'second class justice' but is also symbolic of the importance the state places on the concerns of vulnerable and disadvantaged groups in society.

Third, the shift of the resolution of crimes away from the public sphere of court proceedings to the private realm of reparation and mediation is said to cause tangible problems for participants (Matthews, 1988; Schwartz and Preiser, 1992; Orlando, 1992). The criminal justice system has developed formalised and articulated rules and procedures to protect the rights of the offender and, to a lesser extent, the victim. When responses to crime are removed from the courts care must be taken to ensure that rights are still being safeguarded. Court proceedings ensure that both victim and offender are equally represented in court by representatives fully versed in the law. In the private sphere, this equalising of power cannot so easily be ensured and status differences between the parties may be exacerbated.

Fourth, reparation and mediation projects have been criticised for 'using' victims to deal with offenders and as acting to provide mitigation for the accused (Reeves, 1989; Young 1989; Davis, 1992). The siting, procedures and practices of projects are said to act in the interests of the state, and to a lesser extent, the accused, whilst giving the appearance of paying equal attention to the victim (Brown and Murphy, 1987).

Finally, if mediation is to fulfil the aims set with respect to victims and offenders, the process and the quality of the interactions between the parties are of crucial importance. In a detailed study of the mediation process Davis (1992) discusses the difficulties for the mediators in managing sessions to achieve the best results.

Despite these reservations the potential for reparation and mediation as a constructive approach in criminal justice has been demonstrated; and the concept appears to have considerable support. The difficulties arise when projects operate close to formal agencies and systems.

The legal context of reparation and mediation in Scotland

The Scottish Association for the Care and Resettlement of Offenders (SACRO) project was the first reparation and mediation scheme in Scotland. Before describing the project it is necessary to consider the legal context and the relationship of the project to the prosecution system.

In Scotland police provide reports on people alleged to have committed crimes to the public prosecutors, the procurators fiscal. The fiscals then decide how the case should be dealt with: whether or not it should be prosecuted and, if so, in what court and on what charges. Fiscals have considerable discretion in responding to a report. They are not obliged to take proceedings in court if another course of action is seen as more appropriate (see Figure 1 below).

Fiscals have available a growing range of alternative options other than to prosecute a case. Over recent years there has been a shift away from regarding prosecution as the proper response to all breaches of the law and an increasing emphasis on prosecution as the 'last resort' in dealing with minor offences. The range and number of formal diversion schemes aimed at removing cases from prosecution have grown, encouraged by the findings of the Stewart Committee (HMSO, 1980; 1983) and the subsequent introduction of legislation in Section 56 of the Criminal Justice (Scotland) Act 1987.

These diversion schemes have put alternatives to prosecution on a firm basis in the fiscal service. The need to explore alternatives has developed within the context of increasing demands on the fiscals and courts, coupled

Figure 1
The prosecution process

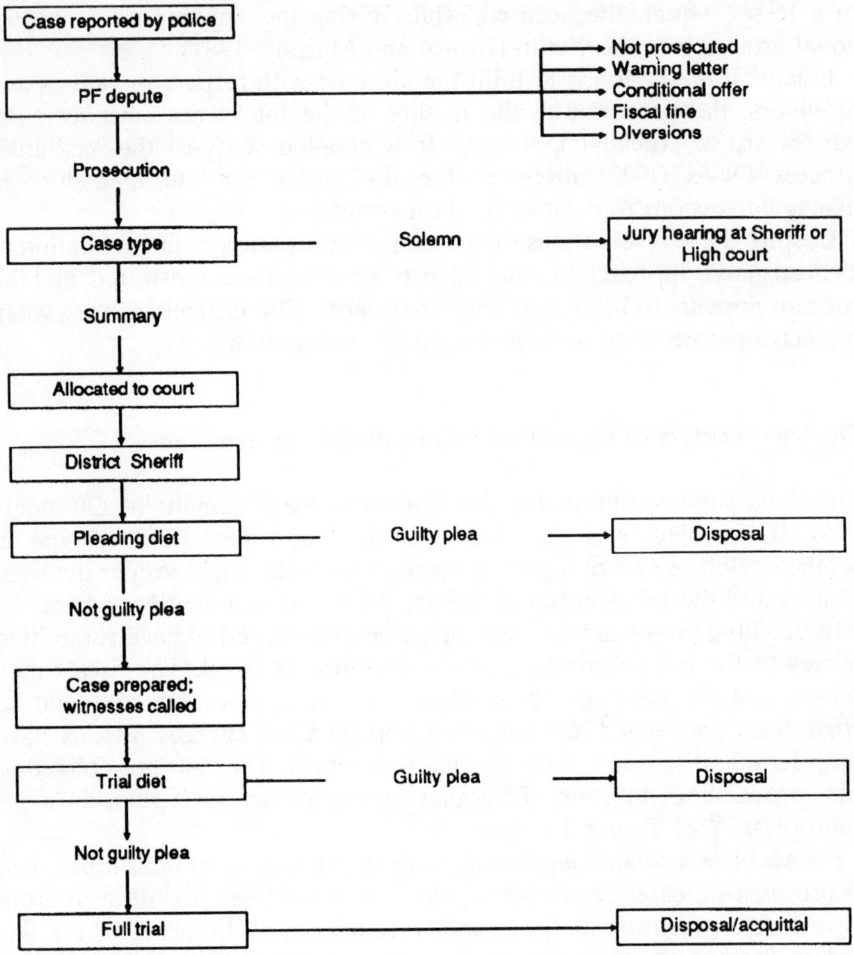

with public expenditure limits. There has also been an increasing recognition that prosecution in court may not be the best way to deal with all breaches of the law and that in minor crimes court proceedings should be used only as a last resort. Examples of this shift can be found in Moody and Tombs (1982) and in a public speech by the Solicitor General for Scotland in 1988. The National Audit Office Report (1989) on the fiscal service showed that the percentage of cases dealt with using alternatives to prosecution increased from five per cent in 1980 to 23 per cent in 1987. This figure includes cases where no further action was taken.

Fiscals also have a further range of alternatives to prosecution. These include monetary penalties, warning letters and formal diversions for accused with problems requiring social work or psychiatric intervention, as well as reparation and mediation.

Referral to a diversion scheme may be made with or without the continued possibility of court proceedings. Diversion schemes tend to operate under the deferred prosecution model, where the fiscal retains the option of prosecution until the accused has fulfilled the terms of the offer. In a few diversion schemes the fiscal waives the right to prosecute when the referral is accepted. In such circumstances the accused will not be proceeded against even if he or she disagrees with or fails to comply with the terms (Cooke, 1989; Stedward and Millar, 1989).

The SACRO reparation and mediation project

From 1987 fiscals in Edinburgh and Glasgow had the option of referring a case to the diversion SACRO reparation and mediation project, one of several formal schemes. The Glasgow scheme has since ceased to operate but the Edinburgh scheme continues. The project operates under the deferred prosecution model and the fiscal retains the right to prosecute until satisfied that the public interest has been met.

The aims of the SACRO reparation and mediation project

The aims of the project are detailed in the two annual reports for 1989 and 1990. These are to:

* Promote reparation as a proper objective of criminal justice.
* Pilot the development of reparation as an alternative to prosecution.
* Test the applicability of mediation as a technique for dispute resolution within the criminal justice system.
* Provide a service to the victims of crime which recognises their rights and needs, and includes an opportunity to obtain practical amends for their loss as well as offering the opportunity to obtain emotional reparation and support.

* Provide an opportunity for offenders to experience a constructive and demanding response to the consequences of offending behaviour that directly holds them to account for their action, without recourse to the court system.

In the initial stages the project had the explicit aim of helping to reduce the pressures on the courts by diverting cases from prosecution This aim was subsequently dropped as unrealistic given the small number of referrals the project can accept in comparison with the numbers of people appearing in court. In 1988 11,588 people accused of offences of minor theft, fraud, vandalism or malicious mischief, petty assault or breach of the peace were found guilty in the Glasgow and Edinburgh District Courts concerned (Scottish Home and Health Department, unpublished figures). In 1989-90 391 referrals were accepted by the project.

The types of cases dealt with by the project

The project dealt with a range of cases and situations involving minor crime. Below are some illustrative examples.

Neighbour dispute

Mr A and Mrs C were neighbours. On occasions Mrs C had been disturbed at night by Mr A playing loud music and banging on the floor. On the night of the offence Mrs C had asked Mr A to keep the noise down. When he failed to do so and became abusive Mrs C called the police. Mr A was drunk and was taken to the police station and charged. After this there were other occasional disturbances.

The mediator contacted Mrs C who said all she wanted was for the disturbances to stop. She did not want to see the accused prosecuted and she was aware he would have problems paying a fine or making financial reparation. Mr A was an older man with a drink problem who had experienced some difficulties adjusting to living in his first tenancy. He was relieved to avoid court and possibly prison and agreed readily to a non-harassment agreement of six months.

The agreement was successfully completed and both were happy with the arrangement. There were no further incidents and Mrs C and Mr A became able to exchange greetings in the close.

Broken relationships

Mrs T had broken the glass in the door of her mother-in-law's (Mrs H) house in an argument about custody of her daughter Mary. Mrs T and her husband had separated a few days prior to the incident and tensions were running high. Whilst Mrs T admitted she had broken the window she denied that this had been done maliciously, saying it was an accident. She thought her mother-in-law and husband had called the police to hurt her but understood this. Since the incident tempers had cooled and Mrs T and her husband had reached an amicable agreement concerning access.

Both parties were happy to accept mediation. Mrs H wanted to avoid escalating conflict in case she lost contact with her grand-daughter. Mrs T was worried a conviction would stand against her if she had to fight for custody of Mary. The women reached an agreement concerning Mrs H's access to Mary and this was successfully concluded. The relationships stayed intact, but there were some tensions remaining. Mrs T in particular wanted to explain her feelings about what led up to the offence and what happened subsequently, but had not suggested this in case Mrs H had withdrawn from the project. Despite this, she was very happy with mediation.

Family dispute

Mr P went round one evening to his sister's house and threatened to break her windows because he believed she had reported him to the social work department who had taken his children into care. Mrs G denied this but her brother threatened to kill her and attempted to break her door down. Mrs G threw her favourite plant out of the window at him in retaliation. The police came, apparently called by the downstairs neighbour with whom Mrs G did not get on. They charged Mr P and also asked him if he wanted to press charges against his sister; he declined.

The victim was happy to participate in the project and asked for a non-harassment agreement and a donation of £25 to a local charity. The non-harassment agreement was successfully completed and helped the family over the Christmas period. However, Mr P moved nearer to his sister and went round to say that he was not prepared to pay the 'sweetie money', and that Mrs G could take him to court if she wanted. This annoyed Mrs G who felt that as her brother was now in employment he should pay the money and that he had had his chance. If he did not pay the full amount she would be happy for the case to go to court.

Mr P had been contacted several times by the project about the delay in payments, but only paid slowly.

Corporate victim

Mr F owned a coach company and his vehicles were not uncommonly the target of criminal damage. Q, a young man with no previous convictions, was charged with criminal damage after throwing a rock at the coach and causing £50 worth of damage. Mr F wanted Q to work for his company for one day and said that if Q worked well he might offer him a job. Q agreed and also agreed to meet Mr F. The mediator went to considerable trouble to get Q to a meeting and eventually managed this. The parties agreed when Q should undertake the work and what he should do.

Q never completed the agreement. On several occasions he or his mother said he was ill and eventually he refused to do the work and the case was prosecuted. Q pled guilty and was fined £50. Mr F was disappointed and thought that the accused should be compelled to stick to the terms of the agreement to avoid letting victims down.

Strangers

Mr E was driving to work one morning when another driver, Ms Z, whom he had not let through, followed him and at the next set of traffic lights got out of her car and began to shout and swear at him. Ms Z then began to damage his car. Mr E was extremely angry about the incident, particularly the fact that Ms Z had tried to blame him and refused to take responsibility for her actions. He was also annoyed that the police asked him 'not to press charges'.

Mr E was very pleased at the approach from the mediator. He was glad to be offered a chance to recoup his losses and had been warned by the police that he would be unlikely to receive compensation through the courts. Through the project he received compensation of £152 and £50 was donated to a local hospital. Mr E thought that a court appearance might have made Ms Z feel remorse for her offence, but had been told by the mediator that Ms Z was very ashamed of her behaviour.

The development of the SACRO reparation and mediation project

Addressing the Reparation and Mediation Conference in Scotland in 1988, the Solicitor General welcomed the SACRO project as the first formal reparation and mediation scheme in Scotland. This project developed from an earlier pilot project established by Robert Mackay and SACRO which was based on a review of the existing literature and an exploration of how reparation and mediation might fit within the Scottish criminal justice system. The pilot project was established following detailed discussions with the procurators fiscal and showed that reparation and mediation was a viable form of diversion in Scotland.

On the basis of the pilot two reparation and mediation schemes were developed, one in Edinburgh in 1987 and the second in Glasgow. The three-year experimental reparation and mediation project was set up with funding from the Social Work Services Group (SWSG), the Unemployed Voluntary Action Fund (UVAF) and from various trusts and charitable organisations. Subsequently additional funding was obtained from the relevant local authorities, Lothian and Strathclyde Regional Councils.

The project initially operated only in Edinburgh with a full time mediator/project manager and a part-time administrative officer. In October 1988 a volunteer co-ordinator was appointed in Edinburgh with responsibility for setting up and operating a scheme using volunteer mediators, as well as taking cases herself. Volunteer mediators began to accept cases in the Spring of 1989. The Glasgow scheme, unlike the Edinburgh scheme, was staffed by a full-time project worker and a part-time administrative worker.

The project staff were accountable to a management committee on which the police and members of SACRO General Council were represented. The Council include academics, SACRO workers and social work personnel. During 1990, representatives from Victim Support and the Family Conciliation Service were invited to attend management committee meetings as observers.

A one-year evaluative study of the project was commissioned and funded by the Scottish Home and Health Department. The purpose of the study was to evaluate the impact of the project from a variety of perspectives as a means of informing policy and practice. The evaluation ran from September 1989 and the project was extended to March 1991.

Outline of procedure and practice

Figure 2 (below) shows the referral procedures and practices involved for fiscals and the project.

Fiscals referred cases to reparation and mediation. Initially the project worker selected potential cases from all those which had been marked for prosecution. These were subsequently assessed by a senior fiscal before being referred. Practice changed so that potential referrals were selected at the time the case was marked and final referrals were assessed by both the senior fiscal and project worker. The senior fiscals were the primary points of contact with the project and were responsible for referral,

Figure 2
The stages of reparation and mediation

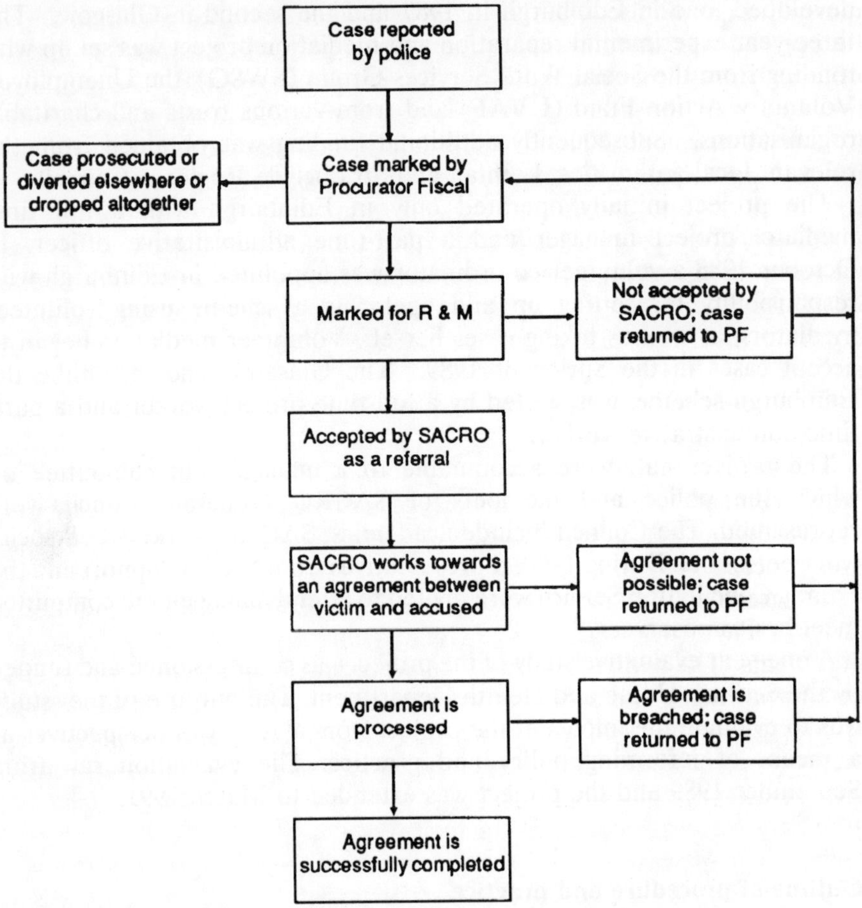

monitoring progress and the final decision regarding prosecution.

Victims were contacted first to avoid the potential problem of the accused placing pressure upon the victim to participate. An introductory letter was sent by the fiscal, followed by one from the project. The letter from the fiscal included details of the aims of the project and explained the right of the victim to refuse. The project letter included the date and time of the proposed visit. Unless the victim indicated otherwise the mediator paid the victim a personal visit to discuss the offence, the project and possible reparation. In a few cases the victim was contacted telephone, either because this was the victim's wish or for practical reasor such as distance.

The mediator relayed the victim's decision and any other relevant information to the fiscal. If the victim accepted reparation and mediation, the accused was sent an introductory letter from the fiscal and from the project. Unless otherwise indicated the accused was visited. The mediator discussed with the accused the offence, their role, the project and the proposed agreement. The accused was informed that the decision whether or not to participate was deemed privileged information; that is, the offer of reparation and mediation was not admissible as evidence in any subsequent court proceedings. If the accused indicated that she or he was not guilty of the charge the case was immediately referred back to the fiscal. The fiscal viewed all agreements made between victim and accused to ensure they were fair to both parties and that the public interest was satisfied.

Agreements could involve the accused in paying compensation to the victim, making a donation to charity, undertaking work for the victim, apologising or making an undertaking to desist from further harassment. The agreements reflected the requests made by victims. Victims were not pressurised to meet face-to-face with the accused and the vast majority of cases proceeded by indirect mediation.

The agreement was monitored by the administrative officer and project worker. Payments were logged and victims contacted at the end of agreements. The administrative officer informed the project worker of any lapse in payments and a reminder letter was usually sent. Occasionally a further visit to the victim or accused would follow. In Edinburgh the volunteer co-ordinator reviewed mediators' cases with the volunteer concerned on a regular basis, and this served as a second check that the agreement was proceeding satisfactorily.

When a case was closed, whether because the agreement had been fulfilled or had broken down, the case was referred back to the fiscal for the final decision on prosecution. Mediators took responsibility for ensuring that both victim and accused were kept informed of progress and outcome.

In April 1990, when local authority funds became available, the scheme in Edinburgh instituted a policy of not dealing with domestic violence cases. This was a condition of local authority funding. No such conditions were attached to funds in Glasgow where the scheme continued to accept such cases.

Both schemes developed close working relationships with other local diversion schemes and resources. In Edinburgh this included liaison with the social work diversion scheme, psychiatric services and the Children's Panel. In Glasgow, there was liaison with the Douglas Inch Clinic and various support services for people suffering from alcohol abuse.

The two schemes operated along similar lines. The main organisational difference between them was that the project in Edinburgh drew upon a pool of trained volunteer mediators whilst in Glasgow all cases were dealt with by one full-time project worker. Otherwise the schemes operated with the same aims and principles and shared the same basic procedures.

The evaluation

The evaluation examined the project from a variety of perspectives, using qualitative and quantitative methods.

Case data

All referrals to the schemes were monitored over a five-month period and these cases constituted the fieldwork sample providing the focus of the research. Details of victims, accused and the offence were collected and fiscals provided information on their final decisions, regardless of progress or outcome.

Qualitative data on the views of victims and accused

All victims and accused contacted by the project during the five-month monitoring period were interviewed or sent a questionnaire to elicit their views of reparation and mediation in relation to their own experience and in terms of its wider applicability.

The comparison group

A comparison group was established in Glasgow. This was composed of cases marked by the fiscals for reparation and mediation and agreed for referral by the assistant procurator fiscal. These would have been accepted by the scheme had resources permitted. Cases were randomly assigned to the comparison group or to reparation and mediation and details of characteristics and outcomes collected. Victims from these cases were contacted and interviews sought.

Interviews with the procurators fiscal

In-depth interviews were conducted with a sample of depute fiscals and senior staff in the fiscal service. They were asked their views concerning appropriate and inappropriate referrals to reparation and mediation; their expectations of the scheme; and their views of its effectiveness and of possible developments.

Interviews with mediators

Almost all volunteer mediators operating in the project were interviewed. Interviews explored mediators' approaches to the practice of reparation and mediation and their views of its impact.

Views of project staff

Throughout the year project staff provided information and views on the operation and development of the schemes.

Observation

Further information concerning the operation of the schemes was obtained through observation of mediator practice on accompanied visits, attendance at volunteer training and group sessions, and attendance at referral meetings between project workers and fiscals.

Costs

This part of the study, undertaken by the Personal Social Services Research Unit at Kent University, involved analysis of project accounts and interviews with project managers and various staff in the Crown Office. The comparative costs of diversion to reparation and mediation and court proceedings are presented in Chapter Eight and references to the costs of reparation and mediation are made elsewhere as appropriate.

2 Analysis of cases referred to and accepted by the project

The evaluation focused on cases referred to the schemes between 1st October 1989 and the end of February 1990. Cases were, where possible, followed from the point of referral to the final decision regarding prosecution. Details of the characteristics of all referrals were collected from police reports.

This chapter examines the characteristics of referrals. There are two points to bear in mind. First, information in police reports related to a specific offence and might not reflect the wider context of the incident. Second, police reports focused on the offence and the accused; data on victims were frequently not available to fiscals. Along with details of previous convictions and previous police reports, where appropriate, these reports formed the basis upon which a case was referred to reparation and mediation.

Cases referred to and accepted by the project

Table 2.1 shows the numbers referred to and accepted by the project during the five-month monitoring period.

Throughout the report, unless otherwise specified, percentages have been rounded to total 100 per cent.

Table 2.1
Cases referred to and accepted during the fieldwork period

	Edinburgh No.	Edinburgh %	Glasgow No.	Glasgow %	Total Sample No.	Total Sample %
Referred	72	100	103	100	175	100
Accepted	66	92	87	84	153	87

During the five-month period, a total of 175 cases were referred. One hundred and fifty three (87 per cent) were accepted for reparation and mediation. Twenty-two cases had been marked for reparation and mediation but were not accepted, for various reasons. In some cases there were too many victims involved to make intervention by the schemes practical or the amount of loss or damage was considered too great or small to justify acceptance. In both Edinburgh and Glasgow the project worker and the senior fiscal discussed cases where doubts existed regarding suitability and the fiscal made the final decision about referral.

Characteristics of cases referred to and accepted for reparation and mediation

Table 2.2 shows the proportions of cases accepted for reparation and mediation where the victims were corporate bodies and those which involved individuals as victims (definitions of these terms are provided in the glossary). The majority of cases in both Edinburgh and Glasgow involved private citizens as victims. Overall a fifth involved a corporate body as victim. Edinburgh accepted a substantially higher proportion of cases involving corporate victims than did Glasgow. Corporate victims included both small and large businesses as well as a range of local authority departments, including Housing, Social Work and Education. These tended to be victims of criminal damage. Five cases where no victims were cited were accepted by the Glasgow scheme. These were cases where offences had resulted from neighbour disputes and all parties involved had been cited as accused in the police report.

Table 2.2
Cases involving individual and corporate victims accepted for reparation and mediation

Victim	Edinburgh No.	Edinburgh %	Glasgow No.	Glasgow %	Total No.	Total %
Individual	39	59	78	90	117	77
Corporate	27	41	4	4	31	20
No victim	0	0	5	6	5	3
Total cases	66	100	87	100	153	100

Table 2.3 shows the numbers of individual victims involved in cases accepted for reparation and mediation and also shows the numbers of accused in these cases.

Table 2.3
Numbers of individual victims and accused in cases referred to and accepted for reparation and mediation

	Edinburgh No.	Glasgow No.	Total No.
Individual victims	56	118	174
Accused	70	115	185

Of the 174 individual victims, two-thirds were involved in cases accepted by the Glasgow scheme. As discussed in Chapter Eight, concern had been expressed that the Edinburgh scheme was operating under capacity. Thus not only were more cases referred to and accepted by the Glasgow scheme but, on the basis of police reports, these cases involved on average a larger number of victims than cases referred to and accepted in Edinburgh. Glasgow cases also involved on average more accused persons than did those in Edinburgh.

Relationship between victim and accused

Cases involved victims and accused in a variety of relationships. These are shown in Table 2.4. Corporate victims have been included in the 'no relation' category.

Table 2.4
Victims' relationship to accused (by case)

	Edinburgh No. Cases	%	Glasgow No. Cases	%	Total No. Cases	%
Neighbour	18	27	39	45	57	37
Family member	6	9	20	23	26	17
Ex-partner	7	11	7	8	14	9
Friend	0	-	4	5	4	3
Through work	3	5	2	2	5	3
Local shop staff	0	-	2	2	2	1
Unknown	0	-	1	1	1	1
No relation (1)	32	48	12	14	44	29
Total	66	100	87	100	153	100

(1) includes a total of 31 corporate victims

Table 2.4 shows that, overall, more than a third of cases involved offences arising out of disputes between neighbours, usually minor assaults and breaches of the peace. Disputes included those over noise levels and parking or boundary disputes. In 29 per cent of cases there was no previous relationship between victim and accused. These generally involved criminal damage; often the accused had been drunk and had damaged cars or broken windows. A further 17 per cent of cases involved family members and nine per cent ex-partners, usually assaults but occasionally thefts.

There were clear differences in the balance of the types of relationships dealt with in Edinburgh and Glasgow. Glasgow cases included a higher proportion of offences arising in the context of neighbour or family disputes. These tended to involve more victims and accused than other types of case and this partly explains why more individuals were involved in reparation and mediation in Glasgow. Edinburgh dealt with more cases where the victim and accused had no relationship prior to the offence, reflecting the higher number of cases with corporate bodies as victims and the higher proportion of cases involving criminal damage to cars. In Chapter Eight it is suggested that there are greater savings to the criminal justice system in referring to reparation and mediation complex cases related to disputes.

Type of offence

Table 2.5 shows the type of main offence involved. Main offence refers to the most serious charge, with assault as most serious followed by criminal damage, dishonesty and breach of the peace.

Table 2.5
Type of main charge (by case)

	Edinburgh No. Cases	%	Glasgow No. Cases	%	Total No. Cases	%
Violence	12	18	44	51	56	37
Criminal damage	38	57	15	17	53	35
Public order	5	8	20	23	25	16
Dishonesty	9	14	8	9	17	11
Other	2	3	0	0	2	1
Total	66	100	87	100	153	100

Overall two-thirds of cases concerned violence or criminal damage. The majority of cases in Edinburgh involved criminal damage; in Glasgow, they were principally violence. Glasgow also dealt with a higher proportion of public order offences.

Characteristics of victims and accused in cases accepted by the project

Victims

Table 2.6 shows the sex and employment status of victims in cases accepted for reparation and mediation.

Table 2.6
Characteristics of individual victims

	Edinburgh No. Victims	%	Glasgow No. Victims	%	Total No. Victims	%
Sex						
Women	24	43	71	60	95	55
Men	32	57	47	40	79	45
Total	56	100	118	100	174	100
Employment status						
Employed	33	59	43	36	76	44
Unemployed	3	5	5	4	8	4
Housewife(1)	7	13	9	8	16	9
In education	7	13	8	7	15	9
Retired	3	5	4	3	7	4
Other	3	5	0	-	3	2
Not known	0	-	49	42	49	28
Total	56	100	118	100	174	100

(1) 'Housewife' is the term used in police reports.

Over half the victims were women, but in Edinburgh there were more men than women victims. On the information available most victims were employed, although data were missing for almost half the victims in Glasgow.

Table 2.6 also reveals some interesting gender differences. Women were more likely than men to be victims in cases where offences arose from family disputes; 24 per cent of women victims compared with 14 per cent of men victims had been involved in such cases. In one example a daughter was charged with stealing from her mother's purse. Mother and daughter had a difficult relationship and this was not the first time such an incident had occurred. The mother had reached the end of her tether and called the police. In another case an argument between two brothers led to the mother becoming so frightened that she called the police.

Women were also more likely to be victims when the accused was a former partner or where the offence related to a previous relationship. It was not unusual for these offences to be related to access to the children of the partnership. The father might have objected to the mother's new relationship or have feared loss of access to the child. Thirteen per cent of women compared with five per cent of men were victims in such circumstances. The difference was more marked in Edinburgh, where 21 per cent of women were victims in cases where the accused was an ex-partner.

Men were more likely than women to be the victim in cases where there was no prior relationship between victim and accused. More than 25 per cent of men compared with 11 per cent of women were victims in such a context. In Edinburgh 44 per cent of men and 33 per cent of women victims did not previously know the accused. In Glasgow the comparable figures were 13 per cent of men and three per cent of women.

Table 2.7 below provides details of the ages of victims in cases referred to and accepted for reparation and mediation in Edinburgh and Glasgow.

The majority of victims were aged between 16 and 40 years. Glasgow cases involved a higher proportion of younger victims, and this is reflected in the lower mean age of victims in Glasgow. Victims ranged in age from 18 months (the son of one of the parties in a neighbour dispute) to 76 years.

Table 2.7
Age distribution of victims referred and accepted

	Edinburgh No.	Edinburgh %	Glasgow No.	Glasgow %	Total No.	Total %
Age of victim						
0-15	5	9	8	7	13	7
16-25	13	23	40	34	53	31
26-40	16	28	37	31	53	31
41-60	18	32	17	15	35	20
6l plus	4	8	5	4	9	5
Unknown	0	0	11	9	11	6
Total	56	100	118	100	174	100
Mean age (years)		35.9		30.6		32.4

Accused persons

Table 2.8 shows the characteristics of the accused involved in the cases accepted by the project during the five-month monitoring period.

Overall a third of the accused were women (a quarter of accused in Edinburgh). Almost half of the accused were in employment. Across the two schemes thirty two per cent were unemployed although the proportion was higher in Glasgow. In three quarters of cases there was only one accused, but the proportion of multiple accused was considerably higher in Glasgow (32 per cent) than Edinburgh (4 per cent). This reflects the higher proportion of neighbour disputes dealt with in Glasgow.

Table 2.8
Characteristics of individual accused in cases accepted for reparation and mediation

	Edinburgh No.	Edinburgh % Accused	Glasgow No.	Glasgow % Accused	Total No.	Total % Accused
Sex						
Female	17	24	42	37	59	32
Male	53	76	73	64	126	68
Total	70	100	115	100	185	100
Employment status						
Employed	39	56	49	43	88	48
Unemployed	18	26	41	36	59	32
Housewife	5	7	10	8	15	8
Other(1)	8	11	9	8	17	9
Unknown	0	-	6	5	6	3
Mean age (years)		27.2		32		30.2

(1) Includes students, school pupils and retired people

Table 2.9 shows the types of offence committed by accused in cases accepted for reparation and mediation.

Overall a slightly higher proportion of women had been charged with offences of violence (39 per cent compared with 33 per cent of men). Women were more likely to face charges relating to offences of dishonesty and men to have been accused of criminal damage. In Edinburgh two thirds of male accused had been charged with criminal damage compared with five (29 per cent) out of 17 women. Conversely, six (35 per cent) out of 17 women were charged with offences relating to dishonesty compared with nine per cent of men. The difference was less marked in Glasgow, where a slightly higher proportion of women than men had been charged with offences of public order (36 per cent compared with 30 per cent of men). In Glasgow, as in Edinburgh, a higher proportion of men had been charged with criminal damage (19 per cent of men compared with 9 per cent of women).

Table 2.9
Type of offence by sex of accused

Type of Main Offence	Edinburgh Female No.	%	Edinburgh Male No.	%	Glasgow Female No.	%	Glasgow Male No.	%	Total Female No.	%	Total Male No.	%
Violence	3	18	9	17	20	48	33	45	23	39	42	33
Public order	2	12	4	8	15	36	22	30	17	29	26	21
Criminal damage	5	29	35	66	4	9	14	19	9	15	49	39
Dishonesty	6	35	5	9	3	7	4	6	9	15	9	7
Other	1	6	0	0	0	0	0	0	1	2	0	0
Total	17	100	53	100	42	100	73	100	50	100	126	100

Table 2.10 shows the proportion of accused with no previous convictions. Excluded are four cases in Glasgow where details of the accused person's previous criminal history were missing.

Table 2.10
Proportion of women and men with no previous convictions

	Edinburgh No.	%(1)	Glasgow No.	%	Total No.	%
Female	13	76	25	60	38	64
Male	40	75	33	45	77	61
Total	53	76	58	50	115	62

(1) Percentages are based on all cases and so do not total 100%

The majority of accused (62 per cent) had no previous convictions with women marginally more likely than men to be first offenders. There were differences between the projects: whilst three quarters of accused in Edinburgh had no previous convictions, in Glasgow only 60 per cent of women and 45 per cent of men were first offenders.

Table 2.11
Proportions of women and men accused facing single or multiple charges in current offence

Charges	Edinburgh No.	Edinburgh %	Glasgow No.	Glasgow %	Total No.	Total %
Single charge						
Female	15	88	33	79	48	81
Male	31	58	45	62	76	60
Total	46	66	78	68	124	67
Two charges						
Female	2	12	6	14	8	14
Male	18	34	19	26	37	30
Total	20	28	25	22	45	24
Three plus charges						
Female	0	0	3	7	3	5
Male	4	8	9	12	13	10
Total	4	6	12	10	16	9
Total no. accused						
Female	17		42		59	
Male	53		73		126	
Total	70		115		185	

Table 2.11 shows the percentages of women and men accused facing single and multiple charges in the current case. It also shows that in both Edinburgh and Glasgow women were more likely than men to be facing a single charge. The difference was more marked in Edinburgh.

Financial loss to victims

Table 2.12 shows the range of loss or damage sustained by victims in cases accepted for reparation and mediation. Overall victims sustained losses of over £9,000. The sums involved were substantially greater in Edinburgh, and criminal damage cases involved greater financial loss to victims than did offences involving dishonesty. The offences were generally minor. Criminal damage often involved varying amounts of damage to cars, ranging from damage to an aeriel (about £20) to extensive damage to body work, tyres slashed or paint thrown over the car, which could involve substantial sums. Some accused had been drunk or angry and caused damage indiscriminately, for example damaging several cars in the street on the way home from a night out.

Damage to property was frequently caused in the course of an argument arising out of anger or frustration. The accused might have stormed out and slammed a door breaking a window; damaged doors attempting to get in or to get the victim to answer. The cost of the damage tended to be low, between £20 and £50.

Assaults varied both in the amount of injury sustained by the victim and the degree of threat or intention to harm on the part of the accused. In some cases the accused had pushed the victim out of the way or grabbed hold of the victim. Sometimes slapping or punching were involved. Generally victims were shocked and bruised rather than having sustained any serious harm.

Public order charges generally related to shouting and swearing and sometimes issuing threats to the victim. Some accused were drunk; some were making excessive noise at unsocial hours. The nuisance behaviour had often occurred for some time prior to the current incident and the police had often been called in the past. The relationship between the parties was usually tense and escalating and the dispute could have very adverse effects on the quality of life of the parties.

Finally, the dishonesty cases tended to be opportunistic rather than premeditated. In some instances the accused had stolen the victim's purse; others had misappropriated or altered cheques. Offences involved strangers, family and friends and ranged from £11 to £500.

Table 2.12
Financial loss to victims in Edinburgh and Glasgow by type of offence

Type of offence	Loss (£)	Edinburgh No. cases	Glasgow No. cases	Total No. cases
Criminal damage	0-10	1	0	0
	11-25	1	1	2
	26-40	6	1	7
	41-60	6	0	6
	61-80	8	0	8
	81-100	1	2	3
	100-200	7	3	10
	201-300	5	1	6
	300+	2	2	4
Missing cases		21	5	26
		£	£	£
	Min. loss	8	25	8
	Max. loss	450	1,000	1,000
	Total	4,688	2,479	7,167
		No. cases	No. cases	No. cases
Dishonesty				
	0-10	0	4	4
	11-25	2	1	3
	26-40	1	0	1
	41-60	2	0	2
	61-80	0	1	1
	81-100	0	0	0
	101-200	0	0	0
	201-300	0	0	0
	300+	4	0	4
Missing cases		5	3	8
		£	£	£
	Min. loss	11	1	1
	Max. loss	560	63	560
	Total	1,949	98	2,046
Total financial loss		6,637	2,576	9,213

Summary

In the five-month monitoring period 153 cases were accepted by the project. Over three quarters involved individual victims, the remainder, public and private organisations. More than a third of the cases were related to neighbour disputes and 17 per cent to disputes between family members. Women were more likely than men to be the victims of offences related to family disputes and those where the accused was an ex-partner. Men were more likely to be victims where the accused was a stranger. Thirty per cent of victims had no prior relationship with the accused; many of these cases involved corporate victims. Most accused were first offenders, facing a single charge.

Over two thirds of cases involved violent offences or criminal damage; 16 per cent, offences of public order and 11 per cent, dishonesty. Loss to the victims exceeded £9,000. Where personal injury was involved, it tended to be slight and not to require hospitalisation.

3 Progress of cases through the project

The progress and outcomes of cases were monitored on a regular basis by the researcher. Progress of cases through the project was followed until the end of August 1990 at which point project staff provided details of the status of ongoing cases. Details of the fiscals' final decisions regarding prosecution of cases dealt with by reparation and mediation and the court outcomes were obtained from project records or the fiscals themselves.

Data on the progress of cases were collected from the comprehensive records kept by the project. Cases were opened when the project received notification from the fiscal that the victim had been contacted. Case notes included details of visits and other contacts, as well as of the parties involved and the agreement. For various reasons the information in the police reports differed in some respects from that gathered by mediators when they contacted the parties. In cases involving neighbour disputes, for example, the victims and accused detailed in the police report might represent only some of those actually involved in a longer term dispute. Therefore data collected from police reports and from project case records are not directly comparable. Here the term 'case' refers to separate police reports as the schemes dealt with related reports in different ways when allocating their own case numbers.

Table 3.1
Case progress

	Edinburgh No.	Edinburgh %	Glasgow No.	Glasgow %	Total No.	Total %
Referred back after:						
Approach to victim	19	29	31	36	50	33
Approach to accused	7	11	8	9	15	10
No agreement made	1	2	0	-	1	1
Withdrawn by fiscal	3	4	0	-	3	2
Total agreements made	36	54	48	55	84	55
Breach	7	11	4	4	11	7
Part completion	0	-	5	6	5	3
Full completion	24	36	34	39	58	38
Ongoing	5	7	5	6	10	6
Total	66	100	87	100	153	100

Table 3.1 shows that a third of cases were referred back to the fiscal after an approach to the victim. This happened in a higher proportion of cases in Glasgow than in Edinburgh. Relatively few cases were referred back after contact with the accused and in only one instance had the parties been unable to find the grounds for agreement. Three cases in Edinburgh were withdrawn by the fiscal. Two involved counter charges and were withdrawn before the parties were contacted. The third case was referred to the Children's Panel by the fiscal after discussion with the victim. In over one half of cases an agreement was made.

Almost a year after the fieldwork period began nearly forty per cent of cases had been referred back to the fiscal because the agreement had been fulfilled. The proportion of successfully completed cases was slightly higher in Glasgow than Edinburgh. Overall seven per cent of all the accepted cases had terminated with a breach of an agreement. In Edinburgh 11 per cent of cases ended in breach compared with four per cent in Glasgow. In Glasgow five cases were referred back after an agreement had been made but had not been fully concluded. These are described as 'partially completed' cases. Finally, a small number of cases (6 per cent) were still in progress at the end of August 1990.

Cases referred back after an approach to the victim

A total of 50 cases (33 per cent) were referred back to the fiscal after the project had approached the victim. Table 3.2 shows the reasons for referring back at this point.

Table 3.2
Case referred back after approach to victim

	Edinburgh		Glasgow		Total	
	No.	%	No.	%	No.	%
Victim refused	9	47	13	42	22	44
Victim requested no action	4	21	8	26	12	24
No response	4	21	7	22	11	22
Reparation already made	2	11	3	10	5	10
Total	19	100	31	100	50	100

The victim refused

In 44 per cent of the cases which were referred back to the fiscal after an approach to the victim the victim had refused to participate (14 per cent of all cases accepted for reparation and mediation). The number of cases is small, but housewives and victims of assault or of breach of the peace committed by a woman neighbour were more likely than other groups to refuse to participate. Six (25 per cent) of the 22 victims who refused were housewives; 16 (9 per cent) of the 174 victims were categorised as housewives. Usually the refusal was on the grounds that the offence was too serious to be diverted. The victims, and often their children, had been very frightened by the accused's behaviour over a period of time. Court was felt necessary to protect the community and in order for the accused to receive psychiatric or other help.

Conversely only two victims in criminal damage cases who did not know the accused refused to participate; and no corporate victims refused. Usually the offence was one of criminal damage and corporate bodies were satisfied that the accused had made amends in some way.

In cases where victims refused to participate the accused were more likely to be women, to face multiple charges, to be accused along with others or to have previous convictions.

The victim requested no further action

In 24 per cent of cases referred back after an approach was made to the victim the victim had requested that no further action be taken. When mediators visited victims in these cases the situation had often been resolved; for example, the accused in a neighbour dispute had moved away. Some victims reported that they bore some responsibility for the offence and that prosecution would be unfair. Others felt the accused had already been punished for the offence. One victim, for example, reported that as a result of the incident, a long standing friendship with the accused had ended. Under the circumstances prosecution would achieve little other than further bitterness. The fiscal was informed of the circumstances and in all such cases decided on the basis of the new information not to prosecute the accused. All of these cases involved assault, and all but one (a family dispute) were disputes involving neighbours. The cases tended to involve male victims and male accused who tended to have no previous convictions.

No response from the victim

In 11 cases (7 per cent of all cases accepted) the victim failed to respond to the offer of reparation and mediation. This represents a fifth of cases referred back after an approach to the victim. In Edinburgh a higher proportion of men than women did not respond; in Glasgow the reverse was true. The cases all involved neighbours or family members. The accused were all men, most of whom had previous convictions.

Reparation already made

In five cases (two in Edinburgh, three in Glasgow) contact with victims revealed that the accused had already made reparation. In one case a young man paid £300 for the damage he caused to a public building. In another the victim reported that the accused had apologised for the assault and bought the victim a meal to make amends.

Prosecution of cases referred back after an approach to the victim

Table 3.3 shows the outcomes of cases referred back to the fiscal after an approach had been made to the victim.

Table 3.3
Outcome of cases referred back after approach to victim

	Edinburgh			Glasgow			
	Prose-cution	No Prose-cution	Unknown (1)	Prose-cution	No Prose-cution	Other	Unknown
Victim refused	5	1	3	11	0	0	2
Victim requested no action	0	3	1	0	6	2(2)	0
No response	1	2	1	3	1	1(3)	2
Reparation made	0	2	0	0	3	0	0
Total	6	8	5	14	10	3	4

(1) Unknown = outcome unknown
(2) Both involved a warning letter to the accused
(3) The accused was offered a Fixed Penalty

No prosecution resulted in cases where the victims had felt no further action was required or where the accused had already made amends. In two such cases the fiscal issued a warning letter to the accused. In contrast, when the victim refused to take part in the scheme, all but one case was prosecuted. Usually information was provided by the victim which suggested that prosecution would be appropriate. The exception was a case where counter charges were involved and the other party had not responded. As no further offences had come to light, the case was not prosecuted.

Cases withdrawn before an agreement was made

Three cases in Edinburgh were referred back to the fiscal after both parties had accepted the offer of reparation and mediation. Two were withdrawn on the basis of information received by the fiscal. In the third the parties were unable to agree the terms of a settlement. In this case the victim and accused had a professional relationship and disputed payment for work done. They had argued about the sums involved and the accused was alleged to have damaged the victim's door. Both parties believed the other owed them money and the case was returned to the fiscal and subsequently prosecuted.

Cases referred back after contact with the accused

Table 3.4 shows the outcomes of the 15 cases referred back to the fiscal after an approach to the accused.

Table 3.4
Outcome after referral back to fiscal following approach to accused

	Edinburgh			Glasgow		
	Prose-cution	No Prose-cution	Unknown (1)	Prose-cution	No Prose-cution	Unknown
Accused refused	2	0	0	4	0	0
No response	3	2	0	0	2	0
Situation resolved	0	0	0	0	2	0
Total	5	2	0	4	4	0

(1) Unknown = outcome unknown

A total of six accused (four in Glasgow, two in Edinburgh) refused reparation and mediation on the grounds that they were not guilty of the alleged offence. All were subsequently prosecuted. In seven cases the accused did not respond to the approach. Three cases, all in Edinburgh, were subsequently prosecuted. The remaining four, two each in Glasgow and Edinburgh, were not. Details of only one sentence were available, in which the accused was fined. Finally, in two cases in Glasgow where all involved were charged the fiscal was informed that the parties (neighbours) had resolved the situation and the cases were not prosecuted.

Cases where an agreement was reached between victim and accused

Table 3.5 shows the status of cases where an agreement had been made between victim and accused.

Table 3.5
Status of cases where an agreement had been made

	Edinburgh		Glasgow		Total	
	No.	%	No.	%	No.	%
Fully completed	24	67	34	71	58	69
Part complete	0	0	5	10	5	6
Breach(1)	7	19	4	8	11	13
Ongoing	5	14	5	10	10	12
Total	36	100	48	99	84	100

(1) Cases terminated for breach of the agreement

Overall 55 per cent of referred cases resulted in an agreement being made between victim and accused and three quarters of these had been fully or partially completed by the end of August 1990. Thirteen per cent of agreements made had been terminated due to a breach by the accused. The breach rate at 19 per cent was somewhat higher in Edinburgh than in Glasgow where 8 per cent of agreements were terminated for breach.

Eighty eight per cent of agreements had been terminated (successfully or otherwise) by the end of August 1990, when only ten agreements were still in progress. The agreements made between victim and accused took various forms, including financial compensation to the victim, an undertaking that no further incidents would occur, a donation to charity, work done by the accused for the victim, an apology or a face-to-face meeting between victim and accused. Most of the agreements (81 per cent) involved only one component, most commonly compensation to the victim or a behavioural agreement.

Compensation to the victim was usually in proportion to the loss or damage sustained. For example, one accused repaid £500 he obtained by altering the amount on a cheque from the victim, in the belief that this was the sum the victim owed him. In another £200 was paid to cover damage to the victim's car during a demonstration. At the other extreme one accused paid £18 to two victims from whom she was alleged to have stolen; and two young women between them paid the £11 taxi fare they owed. Donations to charity were mainly used in Glasgow and tended to be of the order of £20 to £25. A range of local and national charities benefited.

When the accused made a behavioural undertaking the agreement usually required her or him to desist from behaviour which irritated or threatened the victim or other party. In one complex case three neighbouring parties were involved in agreements about where each should park their cars to avoid blocking each other. In another case the accused was a 50-year-old man who had just moved into his own tenancy and who agreed not to bang on the floor or play music late at night.

Direct reparation in the form of work undertaken for the victim was rare. In one case two young men tidied up the victim's business premises to make amends for the damage they caused to her car during a street fight. In another the accused agreed to work for the victim's company for a day as reparation for the damage caused. Apologies were generally written rather than face-to-face. The mediator and victim would outline how the apology should be phrased.

Direct mediation was used in only one case to help the parties resolve the differences between them which were related to the offence. The ex-partners concerned met together after meeting individually with the mediator. In a joint meeting with two mediators they agreed a contract which dealt with access to their child and met the concerns both had about what activities the child would undertake with the other.

Table 3.6 shows the proportions of agreements made in Edinburgh and Glasgow involving different components. Agreements involving several demands have been included in each relevant category and so numbers are greater than the 84 cases where agreements were made. Of the agreements made, 36 in Glasgow (75 per cent) and 32 in Edinburgh (89 per cent) involved only one component.

Table 3.6
Components of agreements made in Edinburgh and Glasgow cases

	Edinburgh No.	Edinburgh %	Glasgow No.	Glasgow %	Total No.	Total %
Compensation	29	81	21	44	50	60
Behavioural agreement	6	17	25	52	31	37
Apology	6	17	3	6	9	11
Direct reparation	2	6	0	-	2	2
Donation to charity	2	6	19	40	21	25
Direct mediation	1	3	0	0	1	1
Total	36		48		84	

As Table 3.6 shows, 60 per cent of agreements involved the accused agreeing to pay compensation to the victim and in over a third a behavioural agreement was involved.

In Edinburgh 81 per cent of agreements involved financial compensation to the victim compared with only 44 per cent in Glasgow. Conversely, whilst behavioural components were involved in 52 per cent of agreements in Glasgow, and donations to charity in 40 per cent, agreements in Edinburgh only rarely made use of such components.

Table 3.7 shows the proportion of agreements in Edinburgh and Glasgow involving different components by the type of offence. As in Table 3.6, agreements with multiple components have been included in each relevant category and so the numbers exceed the totals for individual categories of agreements made.

In both Edinburgh and Glasgow agreements relating to offences involving violence or offences against public order frequently included a behavioural undertaking by the accused. Criminal damage and dishonesty agreements usually involved the accused making compensation to the victim. Even when the type of offence was taken into account there remained differences in the types of agreements reached in Edinburgh and Glasgow. For all types of offence Edinburgh agreements were more likely than those made in Glasgow to include financial compensation to the victim as the sole component. In criminal damage cases in Glasgow over a third of agreements involved the accused making a small payment to charity and just under thirty per cent of criminal damage cases involved behavioural undertakings by the accused.

Table 3.7
Components of agreements by type of offence

Offence	Edinburgh No.	Edinburgh %	Glasgow No.	Glasgow %	Total No.	Total %
Violence						
Compensation	2	100	10	42	12	46
Behaviour	1	50	13	54	14	54
Direct reparation	1	50	0	0	1	4
Donate to charity	0	0	9	38	9	35
Apology	0	0	1	4	1	4
Total	2		24		26	
Criminal damage						
Compensation	21	81	7	64	28	78
Apology	5	19	1	9	6	17
Behaviour	2	8	3	27	5	14
Direct reparation	2	8	0	0	2	5
Donate to charity	1	4	4	36	5	14
Direct mediation	1	4	0	0	1	3
Total	26		11		36	
Dishonesty						
Compensation	6	100	4	80	10	91
Behaviour	1	17	1	5	2	18
Apology	1	17	0	0	1	9
Total	6		5		11	
Public order						
Behaviour	1	100	8	89	9	89
Donate to charity	0	0	6	67	6	60
Apology	0	0	1	11	1	10
Total	1		9		10	

Termination for breach of the agreement

Eleven cases were referred back to the fiscal as a result of the accused breaching the agreement. The types of cases breached were quite different in Edinburgh and Glasgow.

Edinburgh

Seven cases in Edinburgh were terminated as a result of the accused breaching the agreement. Even though a quarter of accused in the Edinburgh sample were women, all accused whose cases were terminated for breach were men. Six of the seven accused involved in these cases were unemployed compared with 26 per cent of accused in the Edinburgh sample. Five of the seven cases involved corporate bodies as the victim, compared with 41 per cent of such victims in all accepted cases. In two instances the accused had actually met with the victim at the time that the agreement was finalised. In all cases the accused had made some attempt to fulfil the terms of the agreement, and one accused had been offered the chance of future employment with the victim had the agreement been successfully completed. Detailed information concerning the outcomes of breaches could not be obtained although attempts were made to obtain this from computerised records.

Glasgow

Four cases in Glasgow were discontinued because the agreement had been breached. Three of the four accused were men. The agreements breached involved compensation to the victim and behavioural agreements. One accused was subsequently prosecuted, but details of the outcome were not available. The remaining cases were not prosecuted as the fiscal believed that the quality of the evidence had been adversely affected by the time that had elapsed since the offence.

Partially completed agreements

A partially completed agreement refers to a case referred back to the fiscal and subsequently not prosecuted, in spite of the agreement not having been completely fulfilled. In such cases the fiscal was satisfied that the accused had taken sufficient action to remove the necessity to prosecute. All five partially completed cases were in Glasgow. Four cases involved counter-charges between two parties; in the fifth the accused was out of the country. In none of these cases had there been further incidents between the parties and so no further action was judged by the fiscal to be required.

Completed agreements

This section examines in more detail the characteristics of those 58 cases where an agreement was fully completed and compares these with all cases where an agreement was reached between the parties.

Characteristics of victims in completed cases

Table 3.8 shows the proportions of cases where agreements were fully completed in Edinburgh and Glasgow compared to all agreements made. Also shown are the proportions of agreements which involved corporate and individual victims.

Table 3.8
Type of victim involved in completed agreements compared with all agreements made, by case

	Edinburgh			Glasgow			Total
	Completed Agreements No.	Total Agreements No.	Completion Rate(1) %	Comp pleted Agreements No.	Total Agreements No.	Completion Rate %	Completion Rate %
Corporate victim	13	19	68	3	5	60	67
Individual victim	11	17	65	31	43	72	70
Total(2)	24	36	67	34	48	71	69

(1) Completion rate is the percentage of successfully completed cases as a proportion of all agreements made in each category.

(2) Total agreements

Overall 69 per cent of agreements had been successfully completed within 11 months. The completion rate was slightly higher overall in Glasgow, although Edinburgh achieved a higher completion rate for corporate victims than did Glasgow.

Relationship between victim and accused

Table 3.9
Type of relationship between individual victim and accused in completed agreements compared with total agreements made, by case

	Edinburgh			Glasgow			Total
	Completed agreements No.	Total agreements No.	Completion Rate(1) %	Completed agreements No.	Total agreements No.	Completion Rate %	Completion Rate %
No relation	7	8	88	4	6	67	79
Neighbour	1	2	50	16	18	89	85
Family member	1	2	50	2	8	25	30
Colleague	1	1	100	1	1	100	100
Ex-partner	1	4	25	3	4	75	50
Partner (2)	N/A	N/A	N/A	3	4	75	75
Friend	0	0	-	2	2	100	100
Total (3)	11	17	65	31	43	72	70

(1) Completion rate is the percentage of successfully completed cases as a proportion of all agreements made in each category.
(2) Edinburgh did not accept cases involving violent offences against partners who were cohabiting.
(3) Total agreements

Table 3.9 examines the completion rates of cases involving individual victims in Edinburgh and Glasgow by the context within which the offence arose. Note that corporate victims have been excluded (see Table 3.8 above). Completion rates were generally high in most types of case but lowest in cases which involved family members, where under a third were completed. The completion rate was also low for offences involving ex-partners, with only half of the eight agreements in this category being completed.

Edinburgh achieved a higher completion rate for cases where there was no relationship between the parties than did Glasgow. In cases where offences related to neighbour disputes almost all the agreements made were completed. Given that such cases can be expensive and frustrating to prosecute referral to reparation and mediation appears a very effective option. Chapter Eight examines the cost implications of diverting different types of case.

Type of offence

Table 3.10
Type of offence involved in completed agreements compared with total agreements made by case

	Edinburgh			Glasgow			Total
	Completed Agreements No.	Total Agreements No.	Completion Rate %	Completed Agreements No.	Total agreements No.	Completion Rate %	Completion Rate %
Criminal damage	17	26	65	8	10	80	69
Dishonesty	4	6	67	3	5	60	64
Violence	2	2	100	16	24	67	69
Public order	0	1	0	7	9	78	70
Other	1	1	100	0	0	0	100
Total	24	36	67	34	48	71	69

Table 3.10 shows that overall, completion rates of around two thirds were found for most offences, but that there were differences between the completion rates achieved in Edinburgh and Glasgow for different types

of offence. In Glasgow eight of the ten cases involving criminal damage were completed compared with 65 per cent of such cases in Edinburgh. In Edinburgh, the two cases involving violence were successfully completed compared with 67 per cent of similar offences in Glasgow. However, as the numbers involved are small caution should be exercised in drawing firm conclusions from these data.

Characteristics of the accused

A total of 69 accused persons had completed their agreements within eleven months of being accepted for reparation and mediation. This represents 73 per cent of all accused who came to an agreement with the victim. In this section on the accused, all tables are based on numbers of accused not cases.

As can be seen from Table 3.11, a higher proportion of employed than unemployed accused had completed their agreements compared with unemployed accused. This difference was more marked in Edinburgh where 86 per cent of those who were employed and all of the school pupils, students, housewives and retired people had completed their agreements compared with only a third of unemployed accused.

Table 3.11
Employment status of the accused involved in completed agreements compared with total agreements made by accused

	Edinburgh			Glasgow			Total
	Completed agreements No.	Total agreements No.	Completion Rate %	Completed agreements No.	Total agreements No.	Completion Rate %	Completion Rate %
Employed	18	21	86	24	30	80	82
Unemployed	4	12	33	10	16	63	50
Housewife	2	2	100	2	3	67	80
Student	3	3	100	0	0	-	100
School pupil	1	1	100	2	2	100	100
Retired	0	0	-	1	1	100	100
Unknown	0	0	-	2	3	67	67
Total	28	39	72	41	55	75	73

Table 3.12
Criminal history and sex of accused involved in completed agreements compared with total agreements made, by case

	Edinburgh			Glasgow			Total
	Completed agreements No.	Total agreements No.	Completion Rate %	Completed agreements No.	Total agreements No.	Completion Rate %	Completion Rate %
Sex							
Female	9	9	100	15	19	79	86
Male	19	30	63	26	36	72	68
Previous convictions							
No precons.	26	34	76	27	31	87	81
Precons.	2	5	40	11	20	55	52
Not known	0	0	-	3	4	75	75
Total accused	28	39	72	41	55	75	73

As can be seen from Table 3.12, the completion rate for women accused was higher than that for men. In Edinburgh all nine cases involving female accused were successfully completed. The completion rate was also higher in both Edinburgh and Glasgow where accused had no previous convictions (81 per cent compared with 52 per cent for accused who had a previous conviction). Age did not appear to influence the completion rate.

Components of agreements

Table 3.13 shows the completion rates for the different components involved in agreements. Where an agreement involved several elements, each has been included in the appropriate category.

Table 3.13
Completion rate by type of agreement by components involved in the agreement

	Edinburgh			Glasgow			Total
	Completed agreements No.	Total agreements No.	Completion Rate %	Completed agreements No.	Total agreements No.	Completion Rate %	Completion Rate %
Compensation	19	29	66	13	21	62	64
Donate to charity	1	1	100	14	19	74	75
Behaviour	5	6	83	20	25	80	81
Apology	4	6	67	2	3	67	67
Direct mediation	1	2	50	0	0	-	50
Direct reparation	1	2	50	0	0	-	50
Total	24	36	67	34	48	71	69

Completion rates were highest where the agreement involved a behavioural component followed by those involving a donation to charity, but as the numbers involved are small, differences should be treated with caution. It should be noted that where compensation is paid through the courts there are administrative costs to the criminal justice system without the income associated with a fine (see Chapter Eight).

Throughput of cases

An important facet of summary justice is that cases should be dealt with quickly. Speedy resolution of a case is important for various reasons. First there are legal considerations such as the quality of evidence; problems may arise if there is a long period between the offence and any ensuing trial. Under the Criminal Justice (Scotland) Act 1975, Section 331 certain statutory offences have to be prosecuted within six months of the offence or the case is dropped. This is referred to as 'time-barring'. Secondly, evidence from surveys of victims (for example Shapland et al, 1985) suggests that there are negative consequences for the victim if the case continues for some time.

Finally, accused people also benefit from an early termination of the case, both in terms of maintaining the motivation to fulfil an agreement and in ending the uncertainty that the case might be prosecuted. It should be noted that if a case is simply not proceeded with the fiscals do not inform the accused of the decision.

Data were collected on the time taken for cases to be passed from the fiscals, through the project and be referred back. Information was also collected on the date of final resolution if the case was subsequently prosecuted. The time taken for a case to be resolved was calculated by counting the number of working days (excluding weekends and bank holidays) taken from the day the case was accepted for reparation and mediation until it was referred back to the fiscal for the decision on the final outcome. The mean number of days are shown in Table 3.14.

Table 3.14
Mean number of working days from acceptance of case for reparation and mediation to termination and referral back to fiscal

	Edinburgh Mean No. Days	Glasgow Mean No. Days	Total Mean No. Days
Victim refused	19	44	32
Victim non-response	34	29	30
Victim requests no action	47	32	41
Reparation already made	23	27	25
Accused refused	37	31	33
Accused non-response	55	57	55
Breach	91	110	103
Successful	78	81	79

Table 3.14 shows that if either party refused or the victim did not respond, cases were referred back to the fiscal within six or seven working weeks of the initial referral. In the few instances where the accused had made reparation already the cases were referred back on average after five weeks. Where the victim refused to participate cases in Glasgow took on

average 44 days from initial referral to referral back to the fiscal compared to 19 days in Edinburgh. This may partly reflect the policy in Glasgow of encouraging victims who were not sure whether to participate to take time to consider the offer. The victim concerned would then be contacted a week later by the project worker to ascertain the decision.

In Edinburgh cases where the victim requested no action took longer to refer back than in Glasgow. It is not clear why this was so; there were, however, only four such cases in the Edinburgh sample.

In both Edinburgh and Glasgow most cases where the accused did not respond took longer to complete. When this occurred the fiscal was informed and would ask the police to trace the accused.

Successfully completed cases were in the project for an average of four months in both Edinburgh and Glasgow. Breached cases were held for longer in the project than others, and many of these were subsequently prosecuted. On average breached cases were in the Edinburgh scheme for approximately five months and in the Glasgow scheme for six months.

Table 3.15 shows the mean number of working days (as defined above) from the date of the original offence to referral back to the fiscal. These indicate the overall time-scale of cases accepted for reparation and mediation.

Table 3.15
Mean number of working days from date of offence to referral back to fiscal after reparation and mediation intervention

	Edinburgh Mean No. Days	Glasgow Mean No. Days	Total Mean No. Days
Victim refused	75	106	91
Victim non-response	59	85	76
Victim requests no action	87	91	90
Reparation already made	71	83	78
Accused refused	72	89	83
Accused non-response	114	130	119
Breach	159	147	152
Successful	131	145	139

Table 3.15 shows a similar pattern to Table 3.14 in terms of the amount of time involved in cases with different outcomes. Where victims refused or requested no action the cases were referred back to the fiscal on average 18 weeks or so after the offence. Where the accused had already made reparation or the victim did not respond the time involved was reduced to under 16 weeks from the offence. Where the accused did not respond or the agreement was breached fiscals would be considering whether or not to prosecute the offence five and six months respectively after it was committed. Cases which were referred back after completion of an agreement took on average 28 weeks from the date of the offence. The final decision would be communicated to the victim and accused a week or so after this.

For most types of outcome (the exception being breached agreements) cases took longer from date of offence to return to the fiscal in Glasgow than in Edinburgh. Table 3.15 shows that for certain outcomes Glasgow cases took longer to conclude than those in Edinburgh. In Glasgow more time had elapsed between the offence being committed and the acceptance of the case for reparation and mediation.

In Edinburgh a total of 15 cases referred back for breach, victim or accused refusal, or non-response by either party were subsequently prosecuted, all but one in the District Court. Where either party had refused to participate cases were completed in around nine months. In the case of breached agreements the delay was almost a year.

In Glasgow 19 cases were prosecuted in the District Court following the breach of an agreement, a refusal by the victim or accused to participate, or non-response. Where victims had refused, cases were concluded within six months to a year after the offence (9 months on average). Only one of the four breaches had been prosecuted, thus closing the incident, eight months after the offence. The age of the other three cases was an important factor in the decision not to prosecute. In these cases the fiscal judged that the length of time since the alleged offence would affect the quality of evidence. In some cases, involving statutory offences, prosecution was time-barred.

In Glasgow data were collected on a sample of cases which had been marked for reparation and mediation and which would have been accepted by the scheme had resources permitted. This sample constituted the comparison group, discussed in Chapter Four. Analysis of these cases shows that those which were not prosecuted (43 per cent) were closed on average four months from the offence and most were closed in three months or less. For cases which were prosecuted most were completed in eight months, and a third were closed in under six months. In Glasgow cases accepted for reparation and mediation which resulted in a completed agreement took around three months longer than comparison group cases which were not prosecuted and, on average, a month less than those cases in the comparison group which were prosecuted.

The numbers are small but the evidence suggests that breached agreements did delay closure of cases quite considerably, in some cases for up to a year. The Glasgow average figure was less than that in Edinburgh because fewer breached cases were subsequently prosecuted in Glasgow as a result of being time-barred. This delay of course only applied to a small proportion of the cases accepted for reparation and mediation. As discussed in Chapter Six, fiscals stated that the delay involved in a small number of cases was outweighed by the advantages which could result from a successful referral to the reparation and mediation project.

Summary

Fifty five per cent of cases resulted in the victim and accused successfully reaching an agreement and most of these were concluded within a year of the offence. Only eleven agreements were terminated for breach. In 22 cases the victim refused to participate and all but one of these were subsequently prosecuted. In a further 12 cases the mediator conveyed to the fiscal new information from the victim and there was no prosecution. In some instances the victim reported that the situation was resolved or that the accused had already made amends.

Most of the agreements (60 per cent) involved the accused making a financial payment directly to the victim or a small donation to a charity of the victim's choice (24 per cent). In over a third of cases, the accused made a behavioural undertaking. Completion rates were fairly consistent across different types of case, but rates were lowest where the agreement required the accused to make financial payments to family members or ex-partners. Women were more likely than men to complete agreements and unemployed accused less likely than those in employment to do so.

The time taken for cases to be closed after referral to reparation and mediation varied. Generally cases were referred back to the fiscal within four months of the offence where the case was terminated after contact with the victim or where the agreement was successfully completed. Breaches could delay cases further involving referral back to the fiscal on average five to six months after the offence. These cases were generally prosecuted and closed a year after the offence. In some instances breached cases were not prosecuted because the fiscal felt that the delay involved had adversely affected the quality of the evidence.

4 The comparison group

The research design included the establishment of a comparison group in Glasgow. Arrangements were made for half of the cases which were suitable for reparation and mediation to be randomly allocated to this group. In Glasgow there were sufficient potential referrals for this to occur without reducing the flow of cases to the scheme. Information on these cases and details of the previous convictions of accused were collected from fiscal papers. Towards the end of the study the fiscal provided details of the outcomes of cases in the comparison group.

The comparison group had two functions. First, it could indicate the likely outcomes of cases had reparation and mediation not been available to fiscals. Secondly, it provided a pool of victims whose cases had been processed in the traditional way and whose views and experiences could be canvassed and compared with those of victims with experience of reparation and mediation.

The intention was that the comparison group would be built up during the fieldwork period to the same size as the main fieldwork sample. In practice cases were allocated to this group from the beginning of October 1989 until January 1990 when staff and procedural changes in the fiscal office and the Glasgow scheme precluded the further allocation of such cases.

There was no comparison group in Edinburgh and so the findings and analyses presented in this chapter apply only to the operation of reparation and mediation in Glasgow. None of the differences described below were found to be statistically significant.

Characteristics of the comparison group

Table 4.1 shows the categories of main offence involved in the comparison group cases compared to cases accepted by the Glasgow scheme during the fieldwork period.

Table 4.1
Details of type of offence in the comparison group compared to cases accepted in Glasgow during the fieldwork period

	Comparison Group		Glasgow Cases	
	No.	%	No.	%
Main offence				
Assault	19	43	44	51
Public order	11	25	20	23
Criminal damage	8	18	15	17
Dishonesty	4	9	8	9
Other	2	5	0	-
Total	44	100	87	100

The offences committed by accused in the two groups were broadly similar, although there was a lower proportion of assaults and a higher proportion of 'other' offences amongst accused in the comparison group.

Table 4.2 gives details of the type of relationship the victim had with the accused in the comparison and fieldwork groups. Relationships between victim and accused were similar for the comparison and caseload groups. The comparison group included a higher proportion of cases involving strangers, students and ex-partners and a lower proportion of those involving neighbours, family members and friends.

Table 4.3 shows the gender and criminal history of accused persons in the comparison and fieldwork groups. There was a lower proportion of women accused and a higher proportion of accused with no previous convictions in the comparison group.

Table 4.2
Relationship between victim and accused in the comparison and caseload groups

Relationship	Comparison Group No.	Comparison Group %	Glasgow Cases No.	Glasgow Cases %
Neighbour	18	41	39	45
No relationship	9	20	12	14
Family member	6	14	20	23
Ex-partner	6	14	7	8
Friend	1	2	4	5
Through work	1	2	2	2
Local shop staff	0	0	2	2
Unknown	1	2	1	1
Fellow student	2	5	0	-
Total	44	100	87	100

Table 4.3
Gender and criminal history of accused in comparison group and Glasgow caseload groups

	Comparison Group No.	Comparison Group %	Glasgow Cases No.	Glasgow Cases %
Female	14	30	42	37
Male	33	70	73	63
No previous convictions	28	60	58	50
Total accused	47	100	115	100

Table 4.4. gives details of the number of charges faced by accused in the current case.

Table 4.4
Number of charges faced by accused in the comparison group and Glasgow caseload groups

	Comparison Group		Glasgow cases	
	No.	%	No.	%
One charge	32	68	78	68
Male	15	32	37	32
No previous convictions	47	100	115	100
Total accused	47	100	115	100

There were no differences in the proportions of accused facing multiple and single charges in the caseload and comparison groups.

The two groups were thus very similar in composition in terms of the types of offence involved, the relationship between the parties, the characteristics of the accused and the number of charges brought in the cases. The nature of the differences suggests that the comparison group cases might have been regarded as less serious, and so less likely to lead to prosecution. The pertinent differences are the higher proportion of first offenders and the lower proportion of offences involving violence. In addition, the comparison group contained a higher proportion of cases where the victim and accused had no relationship prior to the offence and fewer intra-familial disputes. However, none of the differences between the groups reached statistical significance.

Outcomes and disposals of comparison group cases

Fiscals provided details of the outcomes of comparison cases. Nineteen (43 per cent) of the 44 comparison group cases were not prosecuted. The outcomes of these cases are shown in Table 4.5 below.

Table 4.5
Outcome of comparison group cases which did not result in prosecution as percentage of all comparison group cases

Outcome	Comparison Group No.	Comparison Group %[1]
No action taken[2]	9	20
Warning letter	8	18
Fiscal fine	2	5
Total	19	43

(1) Percentages based on all comparison group cases.
(2) Includes one case not prosecuted after a warrant was issued.

In just under half of the comparison cases which were not prosecuted no action was taken by the fiscal. Ten resulted in the fiscal either issuing a warning letter or, in two cases, a fiscal fine. As outlined in Chapter Eight, such disposals are cheap compared with either reparation and mediation or court.

Table 4.6 shows the outcomes and disposals of the remaining 25 cases in the comparison group which were prosecuted.

In nine of the twenty five cases prosecuted the accused pled guilty at first appearance. A further seven accused pled guilty at the trial diet, their second appearance in court for this offence. In two cases, fiscals did not provide details of when a guilty plea was tendered but the accused were convicted. Five accused were recorded as having registered a plea of 'not guilty', three of whom were awaiting trial. It is not uncommon for an accused person to change the plea to 'guilty' at the trial appearance. In two cases the accused had pled not guilty to the charge (or charges) and not been subsequently convicted. In one case the accused was found 'not guilty' and in the other the case was 'not proven'.

Chapter Eight outlines the differential costs associated with different pleas. The average cost of an initial plea of guilty at the pleading diet ranged between £37 and £332, depending on whether or not legal aid was

Table 4.6
Outcomes of comparison group cases which resulted in a prosecution

Plea	Outcome	No.	% of Whole Group
Guilty plea at diet	Fine	6	
	Sentence deferred	1	
	Admonished	1[(1)]	
	Not known	1	
Total		9	20
Guilty plea at trial	Fine	6[(2)]	
	Not known	1	
Total		7	16
Guilty plea (other)[(3)]	Fine	2	
Total		2	5
No details of plea	Found guilty (Sentence deferred)	2	
Total		2	5
Not guilty plea	Not guilty	1	
	Not proven	1	
	Awaiting trial	3	
Total		5	11
Total prosecuted		25	

(1) The accused was also found not guilty of a charge of breach of the peace.
(2) One accused was found guilty of criminal damage but a charge of assault was not proven.
(3) In one case the guilty plea was entered at court 'at invitation warrant', the other after being 'continued without plea'.

made available. The average for an initial guilty plea was £74. At the other extreme, a not-guilty plea and trial could cost £469, rising to £1,108 if legal aid and adjournments are included. The costs of the disposals need to be added to this. Table 4.6 indicates that a significant minority of comparison group cases pled not guilty at first appearance.

In fourteen of the 20 cases (70 per cent) in which the accused was known to have been convicted the accused was fined, and in a further case, admonished. The size of the fine for offences of violence ranged from £50 to £l00. In criminal damage cases fines ranged from £25 to £200, with the mean fine being £75. In only two cases were the accused ordered to pay compensation to the victim. Finally, all three breaches of the peace resulted in fines, one for £200 and two for £l00. The numbers of fines involved for different types of offence were small but it is interesting to note that breaches of the peace appear to result in fines of a similar size to those imposed for offences involving minor criminal damage and violence.

Interviews with victims in the comparison group

The fiscal provided the names and addresses of twenty comparison group victims who were contacted by the researcher. The response rate was disappointing. Only four replied, two to refuse. Two victims were interviewed. Whilst obviously not representative they do illustrate two potential responses to reparation and mediation and are similar in many ways to the responses of victims contacted by the project. In both cases the accused had pled guilty at court and been fined.

One victim was a corporate organisation whose property had been damaged by two young men. The offence had been reported and the next information the victim received about the case occurred when the first of two compensation order payments arrived. The response to the concept of reparation and mediation was very positive. It was seen as a sensible, fair and humane response to offences of this nature, where the accused were neither serious nor persistent offenders. Had this victim been invited to participate in the project he would have responded positively and believed that the outcome for him would have been the same. The benefits of reparation and mediation over court were that it saved the public expense of a court appearance and was a more appropriate response for offences involving minor criminal damage or loss to the victim. The victim also felt that reparation and mediation was more likely to have a positive effect on the accused by making her or him directly accountable for the costs of the damage incurred.

The second interviewee was a female victim of a breach of the peace related to a neighbour dispute. She would not have agreed to participate because the trouble with the accused had been long standing and directed at her, her family and most of the neighbours. She believed that if she had agreed to participate it would have been difficult to reach an agreement and that even if some agreement had been reached, the accused would not have kept to the terms. The incident had led to the first charges being brought against the accused and court was considered to be the only appropriate response.

Despite her own circumstances she responded favourably to the principle of reparation and mediation, believing it could work with first offenders or when strangers were involved. She had since moved and was unaware of whether or not the case had gone to court but was very concerned to know the outcome.

The comparison and caseload cases

The number of cases in the comparison group is small and so the findings described in this chapter should be treated with some caution. Most striking is the finding that 43 per cent of cases in the comparison group were not prosecuted. One of the two functions of this group was to examine the extent to which cases referred to and accepted for reparation and mediation were, in fact, diverted from prosecution. On this finding alone it appears that a significant minority of cases accepted for reparation and mediation would probably not have been prosecuted. Eight cases in the comparison group were dealt with by means of a warning letter indicating that some action by the fiscal was seen as appropriate; two were given a fiscal fine. However, in nine of the comparison group cases no action was taken.

This is to some extent consistent with the way in which fiscals in Glasgow saw reparation and mediation as operating. They were clear that there were occasions when cases would be marked for reparation and mediation where proceedings might not otherwise have been taken. Neighbour disputes were often cited as illustrating this point. Referral to reparation and mediation was regarded as the most appropriate way of dealing with the case. It should also be borne in mind that because of the higher proportion of first offenders and the lower proportion of violent offences in the comparison group, a lower prosecution rate than in the caseload group might be expected. This supposition is based on the views of fiscals in Glasgow described in Chapter Six.

Net widening of this magnitude is commonly faced in relation to diversion schemes and alternatives of various kinds (McIvor, 1990b). The implications for accused, victims and the criminal justice system are discussed in Chapter Nine.

Summary

Analysis of the forty four comparison group cases revealed that 43 per cent were not prosecuted, a proportion comparable with net widening levels in other diversions. The non-prosecution rate could not be completely explained by differences between the comparison and other cases monitored in Glasgow. In most of the comparison cases the accused pled guilty and was fined. Fines ranged from £25 to £200 and this did not appear to vary between different types of offence. In two cases the accused were required to pay compensation to the victim.

An attempt was made to interview victims from the comparison group, but only two responded. Both favoured the use of reparation and mediation in minor offences.

5 The views of victims and accused

The responses and opinions of victims and accused to reparation and mediation was an important aspect of the evaluation. The project aimed to provide a service to victims, including an opportunity to receive practical amends, emotional reparation and support, whilst recognising their rights and needs. For accused, the project aimed to help them experience a constructive and demanding response to the offence and to hold them accountable for their actions.

Methods and response rates

The views of victims and accused involved in the fieldwork sample were sought, unless the individual had asked to be excluded from the research or had not responded to the offer of reparation and mediation. Two methods were adopted. A decision was made to delay approaching victims and accused in Glasgow until the new project worker had time to become established. In Edinburgh all victims and accused whose cases had been terminated were contacted by the researcher by letter at the end of March 1990. They were offered a date and time when the researcher would visit to interview and were asked to respond if they wished to alter the appointment or if they did not wish to participate. Thirty five victims and accused were contacted at this point.

A number of victims and accused (14) declined to be interviewed and four were not at home when visited. It soon became apparent that this method of arranging interviews was too time-consuming for the resources of the study. In late April 1990 all remaining victims and accused in Edinburgh and in Glasgow were sent a questionnaire and letter, asking them to return the questionnaire and/or suggest a date and time when they would be prepared to be interviewed. Victims and accused were contacted regardless of whether or not their agreement had been completed, breached, or was still ongoing. This was to allow for the return and analysis of questionnaires and interviews.

Tables 5.1 and 5.2 show the response rates for victims and accused.

Table 5.1
Response rates of victims

	Edinburgh		Glasgow		Total	
	No.	%	No.	%	No.	%
Interview	10	16	3	4	13	9
Questionnaire	9	14	7	9	16	12
Both	0	-	2	2	2	1
Other (1)	6	9	3	4	9	6
Response rate	25	39	15	19	40	28
Total approached	64	100	80	100	144	100

(1) Includes letters and telephone calls

As Table 5.1 shows, under a third of victims replied. The response rate was higher in Edinburgh (39 per cent) than Glasgow (19 per cent).

Table 5.2
Response rates of accused

	Edinburgh No.	Edinburgh %	Glasgow No.	Glasgow %	Total No.	Total %
Interview	3	7	3	5	6	6
Questionnaire	7	17	2	3	9	9
Both	2	5	2	3	4	4
Other (1)	0	0	3	5	3	3
Response rate	12	29	10	16	22	22
Total approached	41	100	61	100	102	100

(1) Includes letters and telephone calls

The response rate for accused was lower than that for victims, 22 per cent overall, and lower in Glasgow than in Edinburgh. The response rate can only be described as disappointingly low, particularly in Glasgow. There are several factors which may have led to this. First, questionnaires are often difficult and time-consuming to complete and rely on quite high literacy levels. The questionnaires used in the survey may have caused difficulties for some respondents. It was hoped that parties would agree to an interview in such circumstances, and some did.

Secondly, geographical mobility is quite high, particularly in Glasgow, and some of the low response rate can be explained by this. Finally, discussions with mediators and project staff and previous research, particularly on victims (Shapland et al, 1985; Maguire and Corbett, 1987), suggest that many of the people contacted by the project would want to put the matter behind them. A reminder of the offence coming after the conclusion of reparation and mediation will have been unwelcome to some. For these reasons, non-respondents were sent only one reminder letter.

It clearly cannot be assumed that the views and opinions discussed in this chapter are wholly representative of those who were contacted by the project during the fieldwork period. For example, there were no responses from accused whose case had been terminated for breach of the agreement. There were, however, responses from victims whose accused had not been traced or who had refused to participate; from women and men; from different age groups and from victims and accused involved in different types of offence and different contexts. Whilst it is possible to speculate on the type of victim or accused who chose not to respond and the reasons behind this, the views represented below provide an important insight into the ways that victims and accused experienced reparation and mediation.

Participating victims

Thirty seven victims who responded had agreed to participate in reparation and mediation. The remaining three had declined. Most victims' agreements had been fully completed. Only two victims were involved in breached agreements. Two Edinburgh responses were from victims who were each involved in two separate cases. Where victims responded in several ways, for example by telephone and questionnaire, their views have been counted as one response.

Feelings about the offence and the accused

Most victims had been angry and shocked by the offence where long-standing relationships had been involved, particularly family and friends, and often felt betrayed and hurt. Some corporate victims saw repeated offending as irritating; for others it was treated as a fact of life. In two cases victims were particularly frightened that there might be further trouble.

Feelings about the accused varied but were often particularly strong and negative if the victim already knew the accused. Some victims felt sorry for or understood the accused, particularly if the police had provided information about why the offence had been committed. One victim was particularly angry because at the time of the incident the accused had attempted to blame him for the alleged offence.

Almost all victims expected the case to proceed to court, although a few had not expected the case to be taken any further or believed that the accused would not be apprehended. Two victims had not been aware of the offence; one victim, for example, assumed that the damage to her car had occurred by accident rather than as the result of a criminal act. Most anticipated that the accused would be found guilty. One did not know and one, the victim of a domestic assault, thought that her partner would be found not guilty. When asked the likely sentence the vast majority felt the accused would face a small fine of between £50 and £200. In one case a mother thought her daughter would get probation; and in another an elderly couple believed the accused would probably receive a fine and a four-year prison sentence. Victims in neighbour disputes tended to assume that police action would be sufficient to resolve the tensions between the parties.

Contact with reparation and mediation

Victims were contacted by the procurator fiscal and by the project regarding potential participation in reparation and mediation. Initial reactions varied. Some victims said they were confused since although reparation and mediation was an interesting idea, it was a novel one. The concept appealed to many in principle and, whilst a few were doubtful as to its likely success, all had wanted to find out more. The opportunity for compensation was welcomed by many; however, a few were concerned that the accused would be 'let off' if the amount involved was too low.

Whilst the idea of reparation and mediation stimulated interest victims found it difficult to imagine what would be required of them and some were unclear whether the case would go to court as well. Most victims felt they would not be required to do anything should they participate. One victim believed that she and the accused would be expected to give their stories to a mediating panel but most understood that they would discuss the case with the mediator and the accused would make the requisite payments. A few victims hoped the accused would be counselled for problems and others that the accused would undertake some kind of community service.

In two cases victims were very concerned by the project's contact. One couple said in interview that they had wanted the accused to go to court for the offence (to receive a long prison sentence) and thought they had refused to participate. In the second case neighbours were involved in counter charges so that, in effect, victims and accused were contacted simultaneously. The approach was felt by one party to have exacerbated the situation.

Reasons for participation

Victims by and large co-operated to obtain personal compensation, to help the accused and to benefit the community, without the necessity of a court appearance. Victims in Glasgow tended to regard court as terrifying and in Edinburgh as unpleasant and tedious. In assault cases, where the parties knew each other, compensation was less important than providing the accused with help for their problems. Victims believed this would achieve a more positive response than court.

Criminal damage victims wanted compensation and hoped that reparation and mediation would help the accused avoid the negative implications of a court appearance and a criminal record. Violence and public order victims hoped reparation and mediation would resolve the accused's underlying problems and reduce bad feeling between the parties. Some public agency victims saw reparation and mediation as an excellent way of combining their often conflicting demands. A housing department, for example, had commitments to all tenants including accused persons. Reparation and mediation allowed them to collect money for repairs without the financial and personal costs to themselves and accused of a court case.

Contact with the mediator

Sixty per cent of respondents were very satisfied with the approach from the mediator. All felt the mediator explained the project well and that they could have refused to participate. Five victims reported that they had not had sufficient opportunity to give their story. Two of these had been contacted by telephone and would have preferred to meet the mediator face-to-face: telephone contact had not enabled them to talk about their experiences. In another case the victims in a neighbour dispute felt that whilst they were entirely innocent the mediator had inferred they were in some way guilty.

One aim of the project was to provide a service to victims which recognised their needs and the right to obtain amends and emotional support. The usual practice was for the mediator to encourage the victim to determine the nature and extent of the reparation required of the accused in order to ensure that the victim was satisfied with the way the offence had been resolved. In four cases victims commented that they had not determined the agreement: rather, the mediator had proposed an agreement which was felt to be appropriate. There was no evidence that such victims felt any pressure to participate or to confirm an unacceptable agreement. They did believe, however, that the ideal agreement might have differed slightly from the one actually made, particularly in criminal damage cases where the accused was a stranger. Some victims would have in addition liked an apology from the accused.

Several respondents would have liked the accused to undertake some work of general benefit to the community rather than to make reparation directly to themselves. The possibility of such work had been discussed with the mediator and victims accepted that the project could not undertake such work. These victims believed that the development of such an option would be a useful addition. The project manager reported that one victim had arranged for a small number of accused to undertake such work and had negotiated insurance and union details.

Aims of the agreement

In Edinburgh where the bulk of the cases involved criminal damage, most victims hoped to obtain compensation for their loss without having to go to court. They wanted an agreement that was fair to themselves and which offered the accused a chance to make amends. All of the victims who responded hoped that the agreement would have a positive effect on the accused's attitudes and prevent future offending. Only eight felt that an important aspect of the agreement was that the accused should be punished. Five felt that punishing the accused was not at all an important function of making the agreement. Only five thought it was important that they be involved in decision making in the criminal justice system.

In Glasgow more cases involved violence or public order offences where personal compensation was much less important. In three cases compensation was considered important. In each of these the offences were of criminal damage and the victims did not know the accused. Half the Glasgow victims felt it important to punish the accused and all agreed that it was important to affect the accused's attitudes and so stop further offending.

Views on the completion of the agreement

The majority of victims believed that their agreement had been satisfactorily completed. Four victims in Edinburgh, corporate bodies and individuals, had met the accused. They placed considerable value on having the opportunity to speak to the accused of their feelings and to obtain a face-to-face apology. Most victims, even if they knew the accused, did not want such a meeting, believing that it would be embarrassing or potentially dangerous. Only one victim would, in retrospect, have wanted to meet the accused to explain the impact that the offence had had on him.

Views of the offence and accused after reparation and mediation

Victims were asked whether or not reparation and mediation had had an impact on their views of the accused and the offence, regardless of how far the agreement had progressed. Five of the participating victims in Edinburgh and one in Glasgow felt their views had changed. One victim now felt pity instead of anger; two felt they had a better understanding of why the accused had committed the offence; and two others believed that their relationships were better than they would have been if the case had gone to court.

The majority of victims felt there had been no alteration in the way they saw the accused and the offence. Where no previous relationship existed the accused was often described as a criminal or 'mindless'. Where relationships did exist there often remained strains and tensions related to the offence. Some victims still held very negative views of the accused, regardless of whether or not the agreement had been completed. In the cases involving breached agreements these were often expressed vigorously.

Benefits of participation

The general benefits victims saw in reparation and mediation paralleled the reasons they gave for participation: to receive compensation, to avoid court and to benefit the accused. Some victims commented that the information and feedback received from the project exceeded what could be expected had the case gone to court. Some public officials reported that their agency benefited through participating in reparation and mediation as this enabled them to balance different roles and responsibilities as well as allowing them to act humanely and constructively with respect to the accused.

A few victims saw a wider benefit to the criminal justice system and society of having a scheme which enabled minor, silly or 'social' offences to be removed from the court process. This was regarded as appropriate and as saving money, leaving the courts freer to deal with serious crime.

Drawbacks of participation

Drawbacks were mainly identified by victims who had not reached an agreement with the accused (for example, the accused had refused) or where the case had been terminated for breach. These cases are discussed below. More general concerns were raised by otherwise satisfied victims.

First, five victims would have preferred the accused to have undertaken work of general value to the community rather than to themselves. One representative of a public agency expressed concern that the financial demands an agreement could place on the accused could adversely affect other responsibilities. One victim thought a court appearance might be more likely to make the accused feel remorse. Some victims commented that participation could involve much of their time and another two reported that participating in reparation and mediation had opened old wounds. However, none of these victims would have preferred the case to be prosecuted. Reparation and mediation was still quicker than legal proceedings and was thought more likely to reduce further offending.

Five victims expressed dissatisfaction with reparation and mediation. In breached agreements some victims expressed anger that their time and goodwill had been abused by the accused. In two instances, both neighbour disputes, the parties reported that intervention had exacerbated the situation. Two victims in similar circumstances said they were angry that they were required to adhere to an agreement and that they had been treated as guilty parties when they were the victims. One corporate victim was extremely annoyed that the mediator had failed to inform him that the accused had refused to participate and that the case was being prosecuted.

Only two victims thought the case would have been better dealt with in court. In one case the agreement had been terminated for breach, and in the other one of the two accused was in considerable arrears with her payments. Reparation and mediation was regarded as a waste of time; and the victims involved would not participate in future and would counsel others against it.

Appropriate cases for reparation and mediation

Victims were asked for their views on the general role of reparation and mediation. There was a general tendency to regard reparation and mediation as most appropriate in circumstances similar to their own. Victims were asked about the use of reparation and mediation with different types of offence, context and accused. Over a third of victims thought that reparation and mediation should be used only for minor offences. Of those who expressed a view, reparation and mediation was felt to be particularly appropriate for criminal damage cases (especially in Edinburgh where these formed the majority) and dishonesty (especially in Glasgow). The majority believed that reparation and mediation was not appropriate for assaults and views were divided regarding housebreaking and breach of the peace.

In contrast, the context of the offence appeared less important. Most respondents felt reparation and mediation was equally valuable for disputes arising in families or between neighbours, workmates or strangers. What was more important was that the offence was not serious, that the accused was not a persistent offender and that he or she was remorseful and accepted guilt. A majority considered that the offence should be out of character. All regarded reparation and mediation as appropriate only if the victim agreed.

As far as it is possible to judge from the victims' answers a positive response appeared to be compatible with a range of views as to the operation and aims of the criminal justice system. Some of the victims saw reparation and mediation as an effective sanction as it did not 'let the accused off' but made them directly accountable for their actions. Some liked the way the project 'hit the accused where it hurt - in the pocket', or the way the project offered a sharp reminder that such offences were not acceptable. Other victims saw reparation and mediation as a more humane and sensitive response to accused who were not 'real criminals'. Many liked reparation and mediation because it was a practical, pragmatic and speedy response to the type of offence where court proceedings were not necessary. There was general agreement that the courts should be used to deal with 'serious crime'.

Reparation and mediation did not appear to be viewed as an easy option for the accused, although it did provide them with a second chance and the bonus of avoiding a court appearance and, possibly, a criminal record. Such a chance was regarded as acceptable in the case of 'deserving' accused but not for persistent, serious offenders.

Inappropriate referrals

Victims would not wish to see referred serious, persistent offenders who might use reparation and mediation cynically as a means to avoid court and subsequent sanctions. Serious offences included rape, murder, child abuse and housebreaking. Serious assaults and incidents in which large amounts of loss or damage were involved were also excluded.

Participating accused

A total of 21 accused who had agreed to participate in reparation and mediation responded to the survey (a further respondent had refused the invitation). Ten in total were interviewed, five each in Edinburgh and Glasgow, and two of these also returned questionnaires. In none of the cases had the agreement been terminated for breach and most had been successfully completed.

The offence and feelings about the victim

Five accused could remember little of the offence as they were under the influence of drink or prescribed drugs at the time. On becoming aware of their actions they felt distressed and ashamed, shocked they could have committed the offence. In a further five cases the accused said that the offence had been committed in anger; they had not intended to offend and regretted their actions later. Some thought the victim had some responsibility for the incident and that, while this did not justify their own behaviour, it explained why the situation had developed to the point it did. One accused said she was desperate for money when she committed the offence and believed the victim had also acted wrongly.

All expressed regret that they had committed the offence, but were not necessarily concerned about the impact on the victim. One accused had attempted to make amends since the offence and two had wanted to apologise immediately afterwards. In five cases the offence arose from an ongoing dispute with the victim. Two accused believed that the victim had acted maliciously in calling the police and had been surprised at this response. One accused thought that she should have counter-charged the victim.

Expectations

The majority of accused expected to be charged and taken to court after committing the offence, with the subsequent financial and personal costs. The personal costs anticipated related to future and present job prospects and, in one case, subsequent custody of her child after separation from her husband, the situation which she believed led to the offence. Two young accused hoped the matter had been dropped after being held for several hours in police custody. Three thought they might have to compensate the victim.

Contact from the project

Reactions to the offer of reparation and mediation were almost entirely of relief and gratitude. Few of the accused had heard of SACRO or of reparation and mediation and welcomed the opportunity to avoid going to court and receiving a criminal record. Two of the five accused in Glasgow were puzzled and confused by the letters of contact (accused in both Glasgow and Edinburgh received similar letters) but grasped and welcomed the offer. Most had no clear idea of what would be required of them or the victim. Six expected to meet the victim and two to give their views to a mediatory panel. In Edinburgh, where more accused had committed acts of criminal damage, accused had clearer expectations, believing that they would be required to pay financial compensation to the victim. Only four accused took legal advice before deciding to participate, and one accused discussed the project with a friend who also met the mediator with the accused.

Opinions of contact with the mediator

Contact with the mediator was generally viewed positively and appreciatively. Some had expected a 'telling off' and were pleasantly surprised that the mediator was approachable and fair. Almost all felt the project had been well explained; that the mediator had not taken sides; that they had sufficient opportunity to express their views and that they had a say in the agreement that was reached. Two accused in particular had found the mediator very supportive at a time when they were upset and distressed.

Some accused were critical of the mediator. Three accused had felt pressurised to participate. One stated that she had not committed one of three charges (the one upon which she felt the subsequent agreement was based). Two others thought the mediator had decided their guilt before listening to their side of the story. The pressures also came from the nature of the decision they faced: to participate or go to court. In such circumstances accused felt they had to comply with the victim's wishes rather than risk the consequences of a court appearance. It was not that they denied the offence nor, necessarily, that they did not wish to reach an agreement with the victim. In one case the accused would have welcomed an opportunity to address the underlying issues with the victim. In another the accused thought that the compensation requested by the victim was excessive. Neither raised their concerns with the mediator in case the victim should decide to withdraw from the project.

Reasons for participating

Avoiding court, a criminal record and the potentially damaging effects thereof were not only major attractions of the project but very important reasons for the vast majority of accused choosing to participate in reparation and mediation. Three accused believed that reparation and mediation would provide a quick solution to the incident and two that reparation and mediation provided a better means to resolve the situation than court. Court proceedings were seen as likely to polarize the parties and re-open old wounds which were beginning to heal. Four accused welcomed the opportunity to compensate the victim and one participated because the project would close the incident confidentially.

Opinions of the agreement reached

Very few had had a clear idea of what the agreement might be, even in criminal damage cases, but two thirds said they were satisfied with the eventual arrangements made. A total of seven accused expressed dissatisfaction with the agreement. In one case two co-accused felt that the victim had not requested reparation commensurate with the damage done; she should have made a heavier demand upon them. The others thought that the agreements were less than fair to themselves: one because she was not guilty of the charge related to the agreement; one because he felt the amount requested by the victim was excessive; two thought their victims had themselves committed offences; and one thought the situation was best dealt with through direct mediation.

It was important to most accused that the agreement was fair to the victim. Only those with strongly negative views of the victim disagreed and regarded compensation for the victim as unimportant. These tended to be neighbour disputes where the accused felt the victim had some responsibility for the conflict.

Most accused thought that their own punishment was an important part of the agreement, which is interesting given that few victims regarded this as a significant factor. The importance of punishment was emphasised more strongly in Glasgow than Edinburgh. On the other hand more accused in Edinburgh thought that it was important that they were involved in the formulation of the reparation and mediation agreement.

Amongst the Edinburgh accused all but one (which was still ongoing) had successfully completed their agreements. This exception in Edinburgh and three similar accused in Glasgow had mixed views about the completion of their agreements. Two pointed out that the situation behind the offence remained unresolved; in one case the harassment which led to the offence continued. A third accused had subsequently taken legal advice and stopped payments although she later paid compensation in full. The fourth accused was dissatisfied because the victim, whom he saw as the 'catalyst' behind the offence, had not had to take any action.

The role of direct mediation

Most agreements involved financial compensation to the victim and/or non-harassment arrangements. Two accused in a case of criminal damage met with the victim and were pleasantly surprised by the experience. They had found the victim friendly, reasonable and understanding rather than angry or vengeful. These two young men were particularly pleased that the victim wrote to them, the project and the procurator fiscal to say how pleased she was with the work they did.

Some accused would have welcomed an opportunity to meet with the victim. If relationships remained strained, the accused wanted to meet to resolve the underlying problems. Two other accused involved in the same case had no previous relationship with the victim prior to the offence but would have welcomed the opportunity to apologise to her face-to-face, to explain their actions and to show the victim they were not the thoughtless, violent individuals they assumed she saw them to be.

Expectations of court

Six accused had previous experience of court, which had been traumatic, unpleasant and time-consuming. Those without such experience thought it would be frightening and some that it would be embarrassing and humiliating for themselves and their families. Accused expressed more concern about the court appearance and conviction than about any sentence which might be imposed.

Most accused would not have preferred a court appearance, although two had mixed feelings. Both felt that the victim was not entirely blameless and that the victim's responsibilities would have been brought out publicly in court. Others felt that reparation and mediation, through compensating the victim, was the ideal way to resolve the situation and the most sensible and effective response to the offence. One believed that a court hearing would have damaged the fragile relationship the parties were rebuilding. Two accused in neighbour disputes would have liked some investigation into the circumstances and history of the offence before a decision was made about prosecution.

Most of the accused expected they would be found guilty in court and fined. One said he would be found not guilty and another was not sure. Two thought the court would require compensation to the victim and one young man anticipated a 30-day prison sentence.

Impact of reparation and mediation on the accused's views

Accused persons in Edinburgh were more likely than those in Glasgow to feel that reparation had had an impact on their views of the victim, the offence and crime in general. Some accused involved in neighbour disputes in both Glasgow and Edinburgh retained negative feelings about the victim. Two others who had committed offences against corporate bodies said their views had not changed.

Most accused felt remorseful and/or stupid about committing the offence. Some accused were guilt ridden about the trouble they caused for the victim and ashamed that they could act in such a way even if drunk at the time. For some, these feelings pre-dated their involvement in reparation and mediation, but for others, developed through it. Six commented spontaneously they had no intention of re-offending.

The project was widely regarded as fair to the victim. It was generally agreed that cases were resolved more quickly than if they had gone to court and that reparation and mediation was more likely to stop further offending. Some accused (one in Glasgow and three in Edinburgh) felt the project was less fair to the accused and thought that it was difficult for an accused person to refuse to participate. Some saw this as an inevitable facet of the situation they found themselves in, but others felt pressurised by the mediator to participate.

Whilst most accused disagreed strongly that the project was a 'let off', four (two from each project) agreed. In interview an accused explained that, compared to her fears of court, any alternative was, to some extent, a 'let off'.

Benefits of reparation and mediation

Reparation and mediation was valued because it benefited all the parties involved. For the accused there were the obvious benefits of avoiding a court appearance and a criminal record. Accused persons felt that most victims wanted peace and resolution as well as compensation in appropriate cases and that reparation and mediation offered this. There was a general belief that courts should not deal with 'silly' and minor offences, since this was seen as unnecessary, expensive and ineffective. For those accused people who felt positive about compensating the victim (most of those in Edinburgh where there was a higher proportion of financial agreements) the project offered a convenient way of making payments and also reminded them of the continuing need to pay until the agreement had been fulfilled.

Drawbacks of participation

Nine of the respondents identified actual or potential drawbacks of reparation and mediation. Three (from Edinburgh and Glasgow) said they had felt pressurised to participate and that they had not had sufficient opportunity to give their version of events. In two of these cases telephone contact was thought to be a factor and it was felt that a face-to-face meeting with the mediator could have resolved this. Two felt unable to become actively involved in negotiating an agreement because they feared the victim might withdraw and the case would subsequently be prosecuted. Three accused raised the possibility that an accused person might manipulate the situation through reparation and mediation and might not genuinely be remorseful. Finally, one accused wondered if the victims felt reparation and mediation was a 'soft option'.

Potential application of reparation and mediation

Reparation and mediation was seen as appropriate for minor offences, first offenders and for 'silly', 'one off' or out of character offences. Perceptions of the severity of the offence appeared more important than the type of offence in differentiating suitable and unsuitable referrals. Criminal damage and theft were regarded as suitably minor, as long as small amounts were involved and the accused was not a persistent offender. Views regarding assaults were mixed. Either assaults were regarded as serious by their very nature and so should be dealt with through the courts or minor assaults would be appropriate for reparation and mediation.

Views were mixed about the suitability of housebreaking and traffic offences. Serious offences such as murder, rape, child abuse, premeditated violence, drunk driving and offences involving a substantial amount of damage or loss were considered inappropriate. Some believed that cases should not be referred if the accused was not remorseful or if the offence was premeditated or wilful. Persistent and repeat offenders were also felt to be inappropriate referrals to reparation and mediation.

There was strong support for reparation and mediation in family disputes in particular. Support for reparation and mediation in neighbour disputes, or in cases involving strangers was mixed. Accused persons generally felt that circumstances similar to their own were appropriate for reparation and mediation.

Seven accused people suggested amendments to the way reparation and mediation operated. Five of these would have welcomed the opportunity to meet the victim, to discuss mutual problems, to apologise and to reassure the victim. Two accused persons stressed the importance of receiving a personal visit from the mediator. Both had only dealt with the mediator by telephone and would have welcomed the opportunity to discuss the case and to air their views. One suggested that a meeting with the mediator should be mandatory. Both appeared to have been left with a sense that they had been badly treated by the project and that justice had not been done. However, neither would have preferred the case to have gone to court. Finally, one accused person in a neighbour dispute felt she would have preferred a mediation panel to look in more detail at the context and history of the offence.

Victims and accused who refused to participate

Very few people, victims or accused, refused to participate in reparation and mediation. Four people in this category agreed to be interviewed but no questionnaires were returned. Three of these cases related to neighbour disputes and one to an incident involving strangers. The numbers are small, but do illustrate the reasons behind the decision not to participate in the project.

Neighbour disputes

Two of the three victims who had refused to participate in reparation and mediation but who were interviewed had been involved in neighbour disputes: both were women. In the third case the interviewee was both victim and accused in a case involving counter-charges. All incidents involved assaults (in the double case, against the interviewee's four-year-old son) occurring in the context of a long-term, ongoing dispute with a neighbour and after many previous incidents from which no charges had resulted. There was no direct communication between the parties and if any further trouble arose the police were called.

The victims all regarded their cases as too serious to merit diversion. Children and neighbours had regularly been threatened and the victims felt that action should be taken against the accused to make her or his behaviour a matter of public record. All spoke of continued harassment following the original incident and feared repercussions connected with the court appearance. Concerns were expressed that relatives of the victims might retaliate if the trouble continued but all nevertheless wished the case prosecuted. These victims had mixed reactions to the project's approach but had been keen to receive further information. Mediators were reported as friendly and supportive, providing advice and reassurance.

Whilst reparation and mediation was regarded as unsuitable in their own circumstances the victims supported the idea in principle and thought it might have been appropriate in an early stage of their own dispute or in other cases where the accused was not 'dangerous'.

Strangers

One accused who had refused to participate was interviewed. He was charged with criminal damage to a car and, until contacted by the police, believed that the car driver was the guilty party. He was extremely angry about the police response. This interviewee had explained the situation to the mediator whom he had felt listened sympathetically to his views. He regarded reparation and mediation as a good idea but maintained that he was not guilty of the offence and that the victim's dangerous and reckless driving should be noted in court.

Summary

A large part of the evaluation addressed the views and experiences of victims and accused who were offered reparation and mediation. Thirty seven victims responded. The majority of victims, both individuals and corporate bodies, were highly satisfied with the process and outcome of mediation, even in cases where the agreement had not been fully completed. In two cases, the victims were negative about the project and the accused. In one, the victim had not been informed that the accused intended to plead not guilty to the offence and in the second, the accused was in arrears with her payments and the victim assumed she had breached her agreement. The majority of victims, however, felt they had been treated fairly and justly and that justice had been done.

Victims appreciated reparation and mediation as it gave an opportunity to obtain compensation from the accused or to have an ongoing dispute resolved while avoiding their potential involvement in court proceedings. Contact with the mediator was viewed positively and victims valued the opportunity to discuss their experiences and the offence. Direct contact with the mediator produced higher levels of satisfaction than if the contact was by telephone. At the same time, some cases were satisfactorily resolved by letter. Some victims suggested that whilst they were satisfied with the agreement, they might have welcomed an apology from the accused. Few victims met the accused face-to-face and most would not have wished to. Where meetings occurred, the experience was generally more positive than expected.

High levels of satisfaction were also apparent in the response of the accused. Most were relieved to avoid a court appearance and criminal record and expressed remorse or shame at having committed the offence. Some accused people were ambivalent about reparation and mediation, generally this was related to a feeling that the victim's wrongdoing or responsibility for the offence had not been acknowledged. However, in most of these cases, the mediator had helped the accused accept that in spite of their views as to where the blame lay, the decision regarding participation in reparation and mediation was in their best interests. Dissatisfied accused persons reported that the mediator had pressurised them to participate, that they had had no opportunity to discuss their side of the story or said the mediator had assumed their guilt.

There was a broad consensus amongst victims and accused persons that reparation and mediation was a fair and just alternative to prosecution for minor offences. Reparation and mediation was not regarded as appropriate for serious offences or offenders: for example where the victim was a child or vulnerable person; the victim had sustained serious injury or substantial loss; where the offence was sexual or the accused was a serious or persistent offender. Views were mixed as to whether housebreaking should be dealt with through reparation and mediation.

The victims who had refused to participate in the project had all been involved in offences related to neighbour disputes and saw the offence as serious since children had been at risk and the accused had persistently harassed themselves and others. Court proceedings were regarded as a means of ensuring that the accused's behaviour became a matter of public record and repeated convictions would lead eventually to custody or treatment for the accused. The accused who refused to participate intended to plead not guilty to the offence. All victims who refused reparation and mediation were very positive about their contact with the project and felt it an appropriate response to offences similar to those in which they had been involved.

6 The procurators fiscal

Procurators fiscal decided which cases were appropriate for reparation and mediation. The process of referral is described in Chapter One. This chapter examines fiscals' views of the types of cases suitable for referral, their aims with respect to referral and their opinions of the way the project was organised and operated.

Sample and methods

Interviews were conducted with two teams of four of the fiscals who mark papers for prosecution (one team each in Edinburgh and Glasgow) and with six senior staff (three from each office). To provide an indication of how representative the marking teams' views were, senior staff agreed to consult with a wider circle of markers. In Glasgow an analysis of interviews with markers in that office was discussed in general terms with other marking teams. Unless specified the views presented were widely held in both offices by both senior staff and marking fiscals.

The interviews were based on a semi-structured interview schedule which was circulated to fiscals prior to the interviews to allow them to consider the issues to be raised. Interviews lasted from between half an hour to over an hour. They were tape-recorded and fully-transcribed.

The fiscals' views should be regarded as general guidelines rather than hard-and-fast rules. All cases are unique and there will therefore be exceptions to most of the generalisations.

The limits of reparation and mediation

Fiscals would not consider referring cases without sufficient evidence that an offence had been committed by the accused or if the accused denied her or his involvement in the offence. In other cases there was sufficient evidence but the offence was so trivial that no further action was justified. Definitions of 'triviality' varied between the offices, with Glasgow fiscals tending to interpret the term more broadly, reflecting the wider range of cases dealt with by the District Court in Glasgow.

Generally trivial offences involved minor breaches of the peace or other public order offences where there had been no victims, and other offences involving very minor loss or damage. A warning letter might be issued in rare cases where the fiscal felt it was important that the accused was informed that charges were not being brought (if, for example, the accused was elderly).

At the other end of the spectrum were serious cases where fiscals felt there was no alternative but to prosecute. These cases included those in which the offence was serious, such as assaults involving weapons or which resulted in serious injury, sexual offences, and offences against vulnerable victims such as older people or children. Prosecution was regarded as an important public marker of the seriousness of such offences and a deterrence to potential offenders. Prosecution was also regarded as almost inevitable for offenders who had a history of more serious offending showing no break in the pattern or persistence. Those with a history of violent offences were singled out as a group where prosecution was considered important. Prosecution marked public disapproval and repeated conviction built up a record of offending which could lead to the imposition of increasingly serious sanctions. Excepted were cases where the accused appeared to be breaking a pattern of offending.

Other exclusions

Cases were excluded for 'technical' reasons. For example, offences which attracted fixed penalties, such as certain road traffic offences, could not, for obvious reasons, be referred; neither would cases where the fiscal judged that the public interest was best served by referral to other diversion schemes. If the accused had denied the charge, the case was excluded in order to protect the accused's right to prove her or his innocence in court.

Exclusions set by the project

In Edinburgh, funding from Lothian Regional Council was provided on the understanding that the scheme would not accept referrals of offences of domestic violence. In Edinburgh and Glasgow most fiscals were clear that violent assaults, usually on female partners, should be dealt with in court. In most situations it was felt that similar incidents had occurred before and that the seriousness of such offences should be publicly marked. It was considered important that each case result in prosecution both to protect the woman and to ensure that the seriousness of the accused's behaviour be highlighted by increasingly severe court disposals.

Although fiscals were generally in favour of the prosecution of incidents of domestic violence, fiscals in Glasgow did occasionally refer such cases and some of those interviewed in Edinburgh would have welcomed the option of doing so, even if only in rare circumstances (if, for example, previous incidents were thought unlikely and the victim did not wish the case to go to court). Fiscals were clear that none of these considerations alone would be sufficient grounds for supporting referral to reparation and mediation, but would serve as indicators that such a referral might be appropriate.

Identifying cases for referral

Fiscals provided general guidelines for the types of factors which might predispose them to refer a case to reparation and mediation. In most cases fiscals would expect the presence of several factors in a police report before making a referral.

Factors related to the accused

Reparation and mediation was seen as appropriate for three groups of accused. The first were those whose offence was regarded as a 'one-off', a moment of madness. These people generally had no previous convictions and the police reports indicated a particular factor which appeared to have triggered the offence. The likelihood of further offending was viewed as very low and prosecution regarded as being out of proportion to the severity of the case. Being caught and dealt with by the police provided sufficient deterrence and impact while a court appearance and subsequent conviction could have negative repercussions for the accused, far exceeding the severity of the offence.

In Glasgow, unless other information suggested the need for action (such as the seriousness of the offence or the loss or damage to the victim) first offenders were not prosecuted. Before reparation and mediation existed the options were either to prosecute or to send a warning letter, neither of which benefited the victim. Reparation and mediation was viewed as filling this gap in some cases.

The second group of potentially suitable cases involved accused persons with a short criminal record. They were often young people where it was felt that intervention at this particular point might prevent the development of a criminal career. Referral to reparation and mediation had the advantage of keeping such people out of the court system and offered a better forum than court for confronting the accused with the consequences and implications of her or his actions. Through reparation and mediation the accused was required to take personal responsibility for the offence, and with this came the possibility that he or she would not re-offend.

The third eligible group were accused persons who appeared to be breaking a pattern of previous offending. Fiscals recognised that offenders could mend their ways and believed that to use the full force of the courts to deal with subsequent minor transgressions may not help accused to prove their intentions to desist from further offending. Reparation and mediation could not only benefit victims but also remind accused of the consequences of their offending.

The context of the offence and relationship

The neighbourhood dispute. All those interviewed saw reparation and mediation as a particularly useful way of responding to minor offences which arose out of neighbour disputes. 'The stairhead rammy' covered a range of disputes and tensions between parties living in close proximity. Often these had continued for some time and the police may have been called out on numerous occasions.

Court was generally thought to be particularly inappropriate for dealing with offences which arose in such circumstances and the fiscals' dissatisfaction with the previous alternatives open to them is documented (Moody and Tombs, 1982; Stedward and Millar, 1989). It was felt that the adversarial nature of court proceedings could often fuel disputes, re-open old wounds which had healed in the interim, and generally exacerbate emotionally-charged situations. It was also recognised that apparently minor offences in such a context could have serious repercussions.

Fiscals considered that until reparation and mediation became available they had no appropriate formal response to such cases. The potentially damaging effects of a court case might deter fiscals from prosecution, although a response of some kind was considered appropriate. Reparation and mediation enabled them to take action to reduce the likelihood of continued and possibly escalating offending. Whilst fiscals did not necessarily expect the parties to be reconciled it was thought that diversion to reparation and mediation could stop further problems developing and reduce tensions. As discussed in Chapter Eight on the costs of reparation and mediation, referral of this type of case in particular was probably less costly than prosecution. It was also suggested that the accused in such cases would be more likely to plead not guilty, making further savings to the criminal justice system likely.

Family disputes. Some disputes between family members would be considered if violence was not involved. Cases related to disputes between partners or ex-partners were accepted in Edinburgh as long as the parties were no longer cohabiting. Within the family offences between siblings or against parents might be referred as reparation and mediation offered the parties the opportunity of resolving the underlying tensions between them.

Offences involving strangers. Fiscals had differing views as to whether cases should be referred if the victim and accused were previously unknown to each other. Some saw potential dangers in referring strangers. The victim might feel intimidated; he or she might prefer not to have any further contact with the accused; or the victim might resent the burden of having to decide the accused's treatment. In such circumstances fiscals suggested there would be no value to the victim of participating in reparation and mediation. Other fiscals thought that referral of strangers was entirely appropriate in certain circumstances, such as in cases involving criminal damage where the victim had the opportunity of receiving compensation and could choose the degree of contact with the accused.

Senior staff drew a distinction between cases referred with a view to reparation and those thought suitable for mediation. Victims could benefit from compensation whether or not there was a previous relationship between them and the accused. Senior staff also felt that victims were able to make their own reasoned decisions regarding participation when contacted by the project.

Type of offence

Most minor common law offences were felt to be potentially suitable for referral to reparation and mediation. Other factors, such as those discussed above, were generally felt to be more important. Senior staff stressed that as a pilot project, reparation and mediation should be open to as wide a range of cases as possible in order to assess its potential.

Factors associated with victims

There were relatively few factors connected with victims which affected referral to reparation and mediation. This largely reflects the fact that police reports provided few details of victims for fiscals to draw upon. Children and particularly vulnerable victims were the main groups excluded from referral to reparation and mediation unless the offence related to a dispute and was a minor one. Court appearances could be an ordeal for such witnesses and some fiscals favoured the greater human contact, informality and flexibility possible through reparation and mediation.

There were also differing views about the suitability of corporate victims (for example, businesses, public services and large stores). Fiscals in Glasgow were less likely to refer a corporate victim to reparation and mediation as many felt that large organisations might find the process time-consuming and would have little incentive to get involved. Some recalled that in the early days the project manager had contacted some large corporate bodies about reparation and mediation. Whilst those contacted had expressed general interest in the concept they had not felt it appropriate for cases in which their organisation was the victim.

In Edinburgh, with the exception of shoplifting offences from large stores, corporate victims were felt to be equally appropriate referrals as cases with individual victims if other factors involved in the case indicated that referral to reparation and mediation was appropriate.

Fiscals excluded cases with police victims and those in which there were no identifiable victims. One exception was raised by the Glasgow fiscals: these were cases in which all parties in a neighbour dispute had been listed as accused.

The potential impact of reparation and mediation

Fiscals saw the project as serving several ends. These aims were not mutually exclusive and fiscals would usually be hoping to effect an impact along various dimensions. Unlike court, diversion to reparation and mediation offered fiscals the opportunity for fulfilling several aims.

* Impact on accused.
* Compensation to the victim.
* Tackling the underlying problems between parties.

Impact on the accused

Reparation and mediation offered the accused an opportunity to make practical amends for the offence and, once the incident had been closed, to return to being a 'law-abiding' citizen. This was felt to be most useful with the 'one-off accused' and for those described in the police report as having shown evidence of remorse.

Secondly, reparation and mediation required that the accused consider the implications of her or his actions both in terms of possible prosecution and the effect on the victim. This was believed to make accused 'think again' before committing offences in future and was seen as particularly appropriate for younger first offenders and those in what appeared to be the early stages of a criminal career.

Thirdly, referral to reparation and mediation did not preclude the accused obtaining help from another agency, for example social work, alcohol or psychiatric services, either informally or as part of an agreement. In this way the accused's needs could be met without denying those of the victim. This benefit was stressed more in Glasgow where there was a psychiatric diversion scheme in operation at the Douglas Inch Clinic. In Edinburgh a social work diversion scheme was in operation which had good links with the reparation and mediation scheme. As discussed in Chapter Eight very few cases involved such referrals.

Compensation to the victim

Fiscals regarded the victim's needs and concerns as an important element in their consideration of the public interest. Whilst court proceedings offered an opportunity for the victim to receive compensation from the accused, fiscals felt this could be unnecessarily punitive with respect to the accused. Reparation and mediation allowed fiscals to reconcile different interests in such a way that victims were consulted directly about the extent and type of reparation which they felt appropriate.

Fiscals were aware that a court appearance could be an unpleasant experience for victims; facilities for witnesses were often poor and they were often not informed of the progress or outcome of the case. Fiscals were also satisfied that should specialist support or advice be required by the accused, referral to reparation and mediation could be coupled with help provided through voluntary contact with specialist agencies.

Tackling underlying tensions between parties

Reparation and mediation was thought to offer a more constructive means than prosecution of tackling the underlying tensions and problems between parties as they related to the offence. Fiscals felt that reparation and mediation could help parties stand back from a dispute and, even if they did not come to accept the validity of the others' views, at least come to accept that there were differences. Parties could air their grievances informally, without being subject to the constraints of court proceedings and without the associated costs to the public purse. Reparation and mediation could also avoid the entrenchment of viewpoints and positions that might occur as a result of participation in the formality of court proceedings. Mediation offered the opportunity for a controlled exchange of views and the possibility of problems being resolved.

Evaluation of the effectiveness of reparation and mediation

Reparation and mediation was believed by fiscals to offer an opportunity for effective action which would not be possible using other options. Often the cases seen as most suitable for referral were those where fiscals felt the public interest required them to act to balance interests of potentially competing groups. For example, through referral to reparation and mediation an accused could be offered counselling for an alcohol problem and the victim could be compensated without the costs or work involved in a formal prosecution. This flexibility and integration with other resources was felt to be a major benefit of the project.

Fiscal deputes who marked cases felt unable to comment on the effectiveness of the project in practice. In a busy city office markers would not usually be made aware of the outcomes of any cases they marked. The continued existence of the project was taken by them as evidence of effectiveness. Senior staff, however, were aware of the outcomes of the cases, dealt with problems as they emerged and had closer contact with the schemes on an operational basis. They stressed that they were unable to give a systematic view of the project's effectiveness, but did offer their overall impressions.

Senior staff believed that reparation and mediation was effective in various ways. In their experience it was unusual to receive reports of new offences committed by accused during the course of an agreement or thereafter, even though continued offending was far from uncommon in neighbour disputes. Thus reparation and mediation appeared to be effective in preventing further offending in the short term, at least for offences related to disputes.

The project was also thought to be effective to the extent that there was a high level of acceptance of reparation and mediation by victims and accused. Relatively few cases were referred back because one party refused to participate, and only on very rare occasions had a victim contacted the fiscals directly to decline the offer of participation. This was regarded as an indicator of the success of the project.

The form and content of agreements made by mediators were seen as acceptable, and it was unusual for senior staff to make any adjustment. One fiscal noted that adjustments had been more common in the early days of the project and another said that on occasions he might add a short monitoring period (usually three months) to a non-harassment agreement to ensure that the situation had stabilised. Senior staff thought that little intervention by them was required to ensure that agreements were fair to both victim and accused.

Once agreements had been reached senior staff felt the project was generally successful in that most agreements were fulfilled with little disruption. Referral back to the fiscal for breach was relatively rare.

The impressions of senior staff were that the project fulfilled expectations and did divert cases from court. Even though the numbers involved were small, reparation and mediation was felt to be particularly good for cases where none of the existing options had been entirely appropriate. The project was regarded as an invaluable addition, in appropriate cases, to their repertoire of responses, enabling them better to reconcile conflicting interests and thereby enhancing the public interest. As discussed in Chapter Eight there were, however, implications for the workload of senior fiscals.

Reparation and mediation and other alternatives

Reparation and mediation did not operate within a vacuum but as part of a network of responses to offences. The decision to refer to reparation and mediation was made in the context of other options available to fiscals.

Warning letters

A warning letter to the accused would be issued in the least serious cases as a minor reprimand. Usually cases referred for reparation and mediation would be regarded as too serious to merit a warning letter, but two main exceptions were outlined. The first were cases where the mediator had conveyed new information to the fiscal which suggested a warning letter was appropriate. Secondly, prior to the existence of reparation and mediation, the fiscal might have responded to an offence related to a neighbour dispute with a warning letter rather than initiate proceedings which might escalate the situation. Warning letters in such circumstances were regarded, prior to reparation and mediation, as the form of action least likely to aggravate the dispute, but which also indicated that formal note had been taken of the incident. When reparation and mediation became available fiscals regarded this as a more appropriate and effective response.

Fixed penalties and fiscal fines

Fixed penalties were offered in respect of a narrow range of statutory offences where punishment by this means is regarded as a sufficient response (HMSO, 1983). Because fiscals had to offer the accused the option of paying a fixed penalty in certain cases these would not be deemed appropriate for reparation and mediation. A fiscal fine would be considered where the public interest was thought to be best met not by punishing the accused through court but through offering the option of paying a relatively small fine. Since there would be no benefit to the victim fiscal fines tended to be used where there was no identifiable victim or where the loss or damage incurred was minimal.

Social work diversion and diversion to support facilities

In some cases fiscals saw the offence as being indicative of an underlying problem relating to the accused and believed that the public interest would be best served by a response which attempted to tackle the problem and thereby reduce the likelihood of further offending. Cases could be referred on a 'one-off' basis or through formal diversion schemes to resources which were aimed at helping the accused. These included social work support, alcohol programmes, accommodation (for example, hostels), medical or psychiatric facilities.

In Edinburgh, there was a formal Social Work Diversion Scheme (Stedward and Millar, 1989). Cases where the accused would be referred to social work tended to be those in which there was no identifiable individual victim, such as shoplifting from large stores. Stedward and Miller describe in detail how social work diversion is used in Edinburgh.

In Glasgow, fiscals had the option of referring accused to a formal psychiatric diversion scheme, the Douglas Inch Clinic. This diversion was also recently evaluated by Cooke (1989).

In some cases, fiscals were aware that while the accused had offence-related problems which could benefit from specialised help, their main concern was to take account of loss or damage sustained by the victim or to resolve a dispute. In such circumstances a case might be referred to reparation and mediation since an agreement could include acceptance by the accused of some form of support on a voluntary basis. Senior staff referred cases in which the accused would possibly benefit, but where such help was not regarded as essential, since they recognised that the eventual agreement might not involve the accused voluntarily accepting help.

Edinburgh fiscals felt that whilst in theory there were clear distinctions between referral to social work diversion and reparation and mediation it was not always easy when marking individual cases to decide which was the more appropriate. There was often an overlap between the two schemes in that some cases could be referred to either. At the time of the fieldwork the marking team interviewed had not met with the project manager. Such meetings did, however, begin subsequently and may have enabled markers to clarify this and other issues with the project manager.

Opinions of organisational features associated with reparation and mediation

Placing of the project

Fiscals were generally happy with the placing of the project within the voluntary sector. Some senior staff who were best placed to comment on this felt there was the potential for reparation and mediation to be encompassed within the fiscal service, but that this would be impossible given current resources. There were also believed to be advantages of using staff outwith the fiscal service. For example, victims and accused would feel less intimidated if approached by a person not formally associated with the criminal justice system.

Fiscals were asked if they thought reparation and mediation could usefully be operated within a social work department, but there was little support for such an arrangement. Fiscals suggested that locating reparation and mediation there could lead to conflicting demands being placed upon social workers. It was also believed that it was beneficial to use staff whose role and training were dedicated solely to reparation and mediation, which involved specialist skills, rather than to a range of activities.

Use of volunteers versus paid staff

Some fiscals favoured the use of volunteers, others of paid staff, although all saw benefits in both. Using paid staff had several advantages. First, staff would have professional training and standards. Secondly, they would be carefully selected and supervised. Thirdly, it was thought that paid staff would be aware of the crucial importance of confidentiality and would be subject to sanctions should confidentiality or other aspects of practice be breached. Some fiscals believed that the use of volunteers reflected the lack of funding for reparation and mediation and considered that, if money were available, paid staff would probably have been used. However, as Chapter Eight shows, the volunteer scheme was not in fact cheaper than the use of paid staff.

It was also said that, because of their voluntary involvement, volunteers might be more enthusiastic and committed. In addition, several fiscals emphasised the value of having experienced and trained members of the public involved in the criminal justice system; and parallels were drawn with the success of the Children's Panel and the use of lay magistrates.

Most fiscals, and particularly senior staff, had few reservations about the use of volunteers and felt that good selection and training dealt with any concerns. Senior staff in Glasgow were speaking hypothetically since the Glasgow project was staffed by a paid worker; senior deputes in Edinburgh were pleased with the work of the volunteers.

Time scales

Senior staff were concerned that in some circumstances, referral to reparation and mediation meant that a case took longer to complete than if it had been prosecuted. Problems arose in a few cases when agreements broke down some time after referral. If a case was to be prosecuted in court after such a delay the quality of evidence might have deteriorated because of the lapse of time. There was also the problem that prosecution might be time-barred. Thus, if a case was delayed during diversion the option to prosecute might no longer be available should an agreement fail.

In Glasgow the high volume of cases and problems of staff shortages in the fiscals' office, meant that there were often delays in instituting proceedings. As a result time-barring was more of a problem in Glasgow, particularly where diverted cases had been breached and returned for prosecution. However, staff in both offices were clear that whilst delays could be problematic the benefits of having reparation and mediation available far outweighed the occasional difficulties. Delays were already inherent in the system and all diversions involved the risk of further delay.

Administrative procedures in the fiscal service

Some senior staff indicated that internal bureaucratic and administrative procedures in the fiscals' office were based on the idea of prosecution as the norm. Reparation and mediation effectively removed cases from the prosecution flow, necessitating the development of additional procedures, including 'bring up' dates for cases referred to reparation and mediation. There was a feeling that such procedures lagged behind the changes in practice but that methods were being developed to meet the new demands. These procedures did not necessarily increase time delays but did put burdens on professional and support staff in the fiscal service.

Liaison with the project

Senior fiscals and project staff met regularly to discuss new referrals and the progress of cases. In Edinburgh meetings occurred on a regular three-weekly basis and in Glasgow every three or four weeks. There was a preference for regular meetings in Glasgow as fiscals felt that this would better enable them to judge the volume and throughput of referrals the scheme could deal with.

The written correspondence from mediators was praised by fiscals who considered that letters were succinct, accurate and jargon-free. Fiscals were provided with the right information, in sufficient depth. They were happy that the project staff contacted them if there were any concerns and felt they were kept fully informed.

At the time of interview markers in both offices expressed a wish to have some direct contact with the project staff to obtain more information about the project. Subsequent meetings with marking teams took place in Edinburgh and were planned in Glasgow. One senior depute in Edinburgh had also been involved in volunteer training which he had found a useful experience.

Potential development of reparation and mediation

Staff in Edinburgh tended to favour the extension of reparation and mediation to other courts, rural as well as city centre, as there was little scope for increasing the volume of referrals in Edinburgh. As discussed in Chapter Eight, one reason why the Edinburgh scheme was more costly was because it operated under capacity. For the scheme to be viable on cost grounds some way of resolving this would be required.

In Glasgow there was thought to be considerable room for expansion within the District Court even though fiscals were aware that the scheme operated at full capacity. Most markers said they were not referring all the cases that could benefit from reparation and mediation. Cases referred were placed in a tray until uplifted by the project worker. Some markers said that they ceased 'marking for SACRO' when this tray got too full and started again after the existing cases had been accepted. Several also felt that as they became more aware of the potential of reparation and mediation, through hearing about the project, the range of referrals could also be further increased.

Some senior fiscals in Glasgow estimated that the volume of referrals could double or even treble. One interviewee said that it was important that the scheme should receive a range of offences and so he limited the number of criminal damage cases to allow room for those where more mediation was involved, such as neighbour disputes. The numbers of cases where financial reparation could resolve the situation was thought to be under-represented in current referral patterns.

Despite the potential for expansion all were clear that this would not be possible within current resources. Referral to facilities outwith the fiscal service made considerable demands on the time of senior staff who were already hard pressed. Glasgow fiscals were also aware that expansion would not be feasible if the reparation and mediation scheme in Glasgow continued to operate with a single project worker and an administrative officer.

The wider impact of reparation and mediation

Interviewees said that it was difficult to assess the wider impact of reparation and mediation but they believed that it reflected and reinforced recent developments in the way the fiscal service viewed and went about its work.

Over recent years there had been changes in the ways fiscals saw their role, relating to wider debates about the appropriate response to offending and to the development of alternatives. The public interest was not necessarily best served by automatic prosecution; prosecution was now one of several responses and increasingly regarded as a 'last resort' for less serious offences. Several fiscals said that they worked from the initial assumption that the case should be referred unless there was good reason to prosecute. It was believed that this was the direction in which the service was developing.

Unique amongst the options available to fiscals, reparation and mediation allowed them to take into consideration the victims' concerns and to involve them in ways not previously possible. This was felt to be important in that the public interest increasingly focused on the needs of the victims of crime.

Summary

The procurators fiscal who made referrals, monitored progress and decided on prosecution, were highly appreciative of the project. Reparation and mediation was regarded as an effective addition to the repertoire of alternatives to prosecution currently available to them and helped improve the quality of justice.

Diversion to reparation and mediation was regarded by fiscals as appropriate for minor offences where the accused was a first offender; had few previous convictions; or had a more substantial criminal record but had not offended in the recent past. In such cases the fiscal hoped that the accused would benefit from a reminder of the consequences of future offending, but court proceedings were regarded as too heavy a response. Reparation and mediation offered the accused a constructive and active response to the offence as well as being of benefit to the victim. Through referral of appropriate cases to reparation and mediation, the fiscals stated they were better able to balance different elements involved in meeting the public interest including recognising the loss to the victim.

7 The volunteer scheme

As the project became established in Edinburgh a volunteer scheme was set up during 1988 to 1989, building on the practice model developed during the first year. A full time volunteer co-ordinator was appointed in the autumn of 1988 with the task of setting up and running the volunteer scheme. The volunteer scheme was funded by the Unemployed Voluntary Action Fund (UVAF), a central government funded body which aims to encourage unemployed people to become involved in voluntary work. The fund was developed in recognition of the difficulties often encountered in recruiting unemployed people, particularly young people, into voluntary work (Connor, 1989). The role of the volunteer co-ordinator included recruitment, selection and training of volunteer mediators.

Recruitment

Volunteers were selected and recruited in late 1988 and eleven began training in early 1989. Five of this group have since left the project: two moved abroad; two gained employment which they could not combine with volunteering; and a fifth left for personal reasons.

The first volunteer mediators came 'on stream' in March/April 1989 and in September of that year, a second group of nine volunteer mediators was recruited. They began to take cases in early 1990. Two members of this second group subsequently left the project, one to begin a full-time social work course and the other for full-time employment. One volunteer joined the project towards the end of the training course and did not go through the group selection procedure. At the time the interviews were conducted, there were thirteen active volunteers. All but one of whom were interviewed for the research.

Background details of the volunteer mediators

Table 7.1 shows the background details of the thirteen trained volunteers working at the time the interviews were conducted.

Table 7.1
Background details of volunteer mediators

Characteristic	Group 1 Recruited 1988	Group 2 Recruited 1989	All Volunteers
Sex			
Female	2	2	4
Male	4	5	9
Age range			
Min	22	26	22
Max	69	40	69
Mean	42	33	37
Employment			
Emp f/t	1	4	5
Emp p/t	1	1	2
Unemployed[(1)]	4	2	6
Education			
Postgraduate	3	3	6
Graduate	1	2	3
Other[(2)]	2	2	4

(1) Unemployed includes retired, not in paid employment.
(2) Other includes no qualifications.

Studies of volunteers have consistently shown that they are more likely to be women, to be aged between 30 and 40 years and to be from professional and skilled socio-economic groups (Connor, 1989; OPCS, 1982). The SACRO volunteer scheme showed a similar pattern. Volunteer work in the criminal justice system tends, however, to attract a higher proportion of men (Barr, 1971) and this was evidenced here. At the time of applying to the reparation and mediation scheme seven volunteers were in full or part-time employment. Six volunteers were not employed, though not all were necessarily looking for work. Two volunteers later gained employment.

The interviews

Interviews were conducted in early January/February 1990 using a semi-structured schedule circulated prior to the meetings to allow volunteer mediators time to consider the issues raised. All the interviews were tape-recorded and partially transcribed. Since the interviews were conducted volunteer mediators have gained more experience of a range of cases and this may have subsequently influenced their views and methods. The findings should be read accordingly.

Life before reparation and mediation

The volunteers were, by and large, people with considerable involvement in and experience of relevant areas of work, both in paid and unpaid capacities, including the Children's Panel, adult literacy programmes, various residential facilities, citizen's advice or welfare rights and involvement in church and political activities. Experience through paid employment included work with the Advisory Conciliation and Arbitration Service (ACAS), youth work and work in day centres. Some volunteers became involved in reparation and mediation because they had time available, often as a result of changes in lifestyle and/or responsibilities.

Volunteers were attracted to reparation and mediation for various reasons. Many had long term interests in criminal justice and were concerned that it alienated parties, lacked human contact and was ineffective in dealing with many offences and offenders. Reparation was seen as a sensible and humane alternative, making accused accountable for their actions and compensating victims. Some felt reparation and mediation offered the potential for parties to heal the rifts created by the offence and to recover from the incident.

Several volunteers were attracted to reparation and mediation because it was innovatory, offering the potential for radical change in the criminal justice system. The scheme also presented an opportunity to gain useful skills and experience to enhance employment prospects prior to other training, for example in social work. All this could be achieved without having to give up other commitments and obligations.

Assessment of the selection day

Applicants were invited to a selection day which involved various exercises, designed to test a range of skills and aptitudes. These included perceptiveness, communication skills and attitudes, group participation, and handling disagreements.

Volunteers believed that the selection day was an effective way to select potential mediators. The purpose of the day was seen as primarily to 'screen out' those with extreme views, mainly those who were excessively punitive. It was felt the day would select and encourage the interest of volunteer mediators who were flexible and open-minded, rather than 'wishy-washy'. Several volunteer mediators pointed out that selection was a two-way process.

The majority of volunteers were still keen to be involved after the selection day, although some had become aware that being a mediator would not be as easy as they had expected. In interview several commented spontaneously that they had gained a very good impression of the project and of the staff. The volunteer mediators felt the day reflected the extent to which the project was serious and well planned and showed that the staff 'knew what they were doing'.

Training

There were three components to training. First, volunteers attended a series of evening training sessions. These involved outside speakers, role play, talks from project staff and discussion. All found the training evenings comprehensive and relevant. These sessions provided a useful background to the second stage of the training, accompanied visits.

Secondly, volunteers were able to accompany an experienced mediator on visits to victims and accused. The trainee mediators discussed with the volunteer co-ordinator the number of visits they felt that they required before being confident enough to 'go solo'. None felt under any pressure to take on cases alone until ready to do so.

Thirdly, once volunteers had begun to take cases they received a range of in-service support. Volunteers met as a group with the volunteer co-ordinator on a regular basis. This provided an opportunity to share experiences and problems as well as giving a sense of group support. The volunteers also met individually with the volunteer co-ordinator on a regular basis to discuss cases and monitor progress. The volunteer co-ordinator counter-signed all correspondence to fiscals and monitored other correspondence and case records.

The volunteers valued the help and support of the volunteer co-ordinator who was found to be approachable and available if problems or queries emerged, providing professional back up and personal support. Increasingly, volunteers felt they were able to draw upon the support of their colleagues.

Preferences and choices

Volunteers were asked if they would or did place constraints on the types of cases they were prepared to accept or on the time they made available to undertake reparation and mediation. All said they wanted to take as wide a range of cases as possible rather than specialising. At the same time, many expressed a preference for cases where the parties had long-term relationships. Volunteers felt that their involvement in such situations could be particularly rewarding and challenging, helping individuals rebuild relationships.

Cases involving corporate organisations were regarded as less emotionally challenging and demanding than working with private individuals. Most volunteers felt these drew less upon mediation skills but provided a welcome relief from more emotionally demanding cases. At the same time those with experience of mediation with corporate bodies had often found them to involve as much challenge and reward as cases involving private individuals.

Some volunteers said they would be reluctant to take on cases involving domestic violence for personal or political reasons. All were clear that they were under no obligation to accept any particular case.

Undertaking mediation

Cases were usually allocated at the group meetings and volunteers took on as many cases as they felt they could manage. Most volunteer mediators had an afternoon or evening available per week for casework. Only one volunteer reported having substantially more time than this available for work on the project.

For reasons of confidentiality volunteers had to read case notes in the office. Records could not be removed and most volunteers made brief notes of salient points to refresh their memories. Experienced volunteers often went to considerable trouble to ensure that they carried as little information as necessary and that it was as anonymous as possible, even though this involved them in extra work.

After some experience, volunteers tended to form a rough idea of the form and content of an agreement and possible options before visiting the victim, but stressed the importance of staying open-minded and flexible.

Most volunteers adopted the same approach with victims and accused. After introducing themselves and outlining the project volunteers would allow the victim or accused to talk about her or his experiences of and feelings about the offence. In some cases it was appropriate to refer the victim or accused to another agency, such as a victim support scheme or solicitor. Volunteers stressed the importance of reassuring parties that they were under no pressure to participate. Volunteers held different views on the extent to which the accused should be encouraged to discuss the offence and the importance of the accused expressing remorse.

Two broad approaches were apparent. In one the mediator's role was to help the two parties find common ground for an agreement. Here both parties were equally involved in the process of finding a resolution to the offence. In the second, the victim's requirements were conveyed to the accused who could refuse or accept the offer. Some mediators appeared to adopt a particular style in most cases; others varied the approach to the relationship between the parties or their needs.

In most cases mediators found the victim's request for compensation was directly in line with the damage or loss sustained. In assault or breach of the peace cases victims often wanted the mediator to provide examples of different types of agreement. The majority of accused were regarded as satisfied with the proposed agreement. On rare occasions mediators had thought the victim was making too heavy demands of the accused. These cases would be discussed with the volunteer co-ordinator. If it was not possible to reach a fairer agreement with the victim the case would be referred back to the fiscal.

Mediators reported that victims often wanted basic information about the accused, such as age, employment status and criminal history. It should be remembered that volunteers operated in Edinburgh only, where a high proportion of cases involved strangers. It was felt that such information influenced what victims saw as a fair and realistic agreement. This raised problems of confidentiality. As the victim was contacted first the mediator did not know at that point whether or not the accused would accept the offer of reparation and mediation or whether he or she would agree to confidential information being passed to the victim. Volunteers resolved this by offering general information on an accused without revealing his or her identity.

Where victim and accused lived in close proximity it was not unusual, when visiting the victim, for the mediator to find the accused also present. This was not generally regarded as direct mediation; the term tended to be used to refer to formal meetings where both parties had been briefed and a joint meeting pre-arranged and where ideally, two mediators would be present.

Direct mediation was used relatively rarely but mediators would, as was the policy, only raise the possibility with a victim if they could see a purpose for such a meeting. A few mediators would usually ask the victim as a matter of course if they wished to meet the accused, but few victims wanted this. The more recently recruited volunteers felt there was considerable potential for direct mediation in a range of cases and the project manager had encouraged volunteers to make more use of it as they acquired confidence and skills.

Monitoring the agreement

All the experienced volunteer mediators and most of the newer group regarded monitoring the agreement as an important part of their role. The administrator and the volunteer co-ordinator checked payments as they were made and regular case reviews ensured that breaches of agreements were picked up quickly and the volunteer co-ordinator informed.

In some non-harassment agreements, particularly those where the parties were long in dispute, the volunteer mediator may have been involved in several visits. These would focus around discussion of alleged breaches and, if necessary, might involve renegotiation or refinement of the agreement. Often it was a matter of reinforcing an existing agreement.

Breaches. Breaches were tolerated if the accused was believed to be experiencing genuine difficulties keeping to the agreement. Some volunteers were clear that, save for exceptional circumstances, only two breaches at most would be allowed before a case was referred back to the fiscal. For these interviewees it was important to adopt a tough approach to breach in order to be fair to the victim. It was important to stress to both parties that reparation and mediation was not a 'let off' for the accused. Generally victims were informed of any serious breaches and their views on the matter sought. Most victims were felt to be understanding of genuine problems.

In non-harassment agreements there were variations in the extent to which volunteer mediators visited victims to check if the agreement had been complied with. Some would aim to visit the victim at the end of the non-harassment period, but this was not standard practice and some volunteer mediators would write instead. It was assumed the victims would contact the scheme if serious problems arose but that it was important to check victims' satisfaction with an agreement before concluding the case.

The fiscal was generally not contacted immediately an agreement was breached. It was more usual for a case to be referred back after several attempts to encourage the accused to complete the agreement. Some cases were referred back for discussion with the fiscal to ascertain whether he or she was happy for the project to continue trying to achieve a successfully completed agreement.

The project manager confirmed that whilst there was no policy on breach the project was sympathetic to accused who had genuine difficulties fulfilling the agreement. This was particularly so if the accused had made an effort to fulfill most of the demands. At the same time, reluctant accused were less sympathetically treated. Steps were taken to ensure that victims were kept informed of significant breaches of the agreement.

Problems in practice

Volunteers encountered some difficulties enacting their roles as mediators. Some of these are probably inherent in the activity of mediating between parties; others were more easily overcome.

Administrative difficulties

For reasons of confidentiality volunteers were not allowed to remove summaries of police reports from the project office, nor to make photocopies. Whilst appreciating the reasons for this some of the experienced volunteers found the extra work involved frustrating and costly both in terms of time and money. It was felt that other methods could be found to safeguard confidentiality.

Assigning roles

In some on-going disputes, or those where counter-charges were involved it was difficult to place the parties in the appropriate role of victim or accused. Whilst this might be clear in a particular incident, when the longer history was taken into account the roles became blurred, making it difficult to find grounds for an agreement acceptable to both parties. If the concerns were great the case would be discussed with the volunteer co-ordinator and, if appropriate, referred back to the fiscal.

Identifying victims

In some cases it was not clear from the police report summaries who the victim was. This happened in two ways. First, the victim might be recorded as a corporate body, but further investigation might reveal the existence of an individual victim (for example, the tenant of a property). Whilst this could easily be clarified by the volunteer co-ordinator and the fiscal, in the early stages of intervention considerable time could be spent identifying the victim. The other problem concerned locating within a corporate body an individual able to deal with the case. Again, this could be a time-consuming activity.

Assessing motives for participation

Several volunteers found it difficult to assess victims' and accused persons' motives for participating. A victim might participate out of fear of court rather than because he or she felt reparation and mediation was appropriate. An accused might agree to reparation and mediation rather than attempt to prove innocence in court. In such cases volunteers felt they could help the party by discussing in depth the implications of a decision.

In other cases the volunteer felt the accused might participate without feeling remorse for the offence, or a victim might become involved in order to make a profit through participation, that is to gain more in compensation than the loss or damage merited. Little could be done unless an agreement was unreasonable or disputed. In such instances, the mediator would discuss the case with the volunteer co-ordinator.

Verification

Some volunteers expressed uneasiness over the necessary reliance upon the victim's word on matters such as whether or not there had been a breach of the agreement. In rare cases volunteers were concerned that victims might hold the threat of reporting to the project over the accused. Interestingly, only one volunteer voiced concern that the victim might not report an incident through fear of recrimination by the accused.

Balancing the needs of victims and accused

In some unusual cases it was difficult to balance the rights and needs of the victim and accused. Whilst in practice most victims were felt to be reasonable and responsive, some were believed to have made hard demands of accused in their proposed agreements. It was recognised that many accused felt that any agreement would be preferable to court and, for that reason, had complied. Serious concerns were referred back to the volunteer co-ordinator for discussion or referral to the fiscal.

Volunteers' evaluation of the impact of reparation and mediation

Volunteers discussed what they saw as the impact of reparation and mediation. First, reparation and mediation prevented cases going to court where the parties had resolved the situation. Sometimes an offence occurred at a crucial stage in an ongoing problem and prompted the parties to take action to resolve their difficulties. In these cases the mediator could provide the fiscal with verified information (through talking to both parties) and, if necessary, provide victim and accused with support until the situation had stabilised.

Reparation and mediation also enabled victims to receive compensation for their loss without the personal costs attendance at court could involve. In addition, victims were not required to undergo an unpleasant court experience. The accused avoided the potentially damaging effects of a court appearance and conviction, whilst at the same time being required to make amends. Through reparation and mediation it was felt that victims and accused would be better able to come to terms with the offence and to 'close' the incident.

There were benefits for the criminal justice system. Reparation and mediation removed some minor offences from the courts, saving resources for more serious offences. However, it was appreciated that the number of cases involved was small and that there was unlikely to be a substantial impact on the work of the courts. Volunteers felt that victims and accused would see the criminal justice system as more credible through its adoption of a 'sensible' approach to minor offences.

Interviewees were asked what they regarded as the potential benefits and drawbacks of using volunteers and paid workers in reparation and mediation. The initial reaction was usually that volunteers were cheaper than paid staff as the main costs incurred were expenses. In addition, since there was no ready availability of professionals with the skills required by an innovatory project, nets had to be cast more widely and creatively.

Unlike paid staff, volunteers felt they would be much more likely to ask for help or raise problems with the volunteer co-ordinator. Paid staff might feel they should be able to do the job, whereas volunteers were allowed, even expected, to ask for help and advice. Without pressure to perform volunteers felt they could work at the pace demanded by the situation and the participants, rather than 'rushing' them through the system.

Some, but not all, interviewees believed that volunteer mediators were beneficial because they intervened as members of the community and this was thought to be important to victims and accused. Through the social contacts of the volunteers it was felt that the concept of reparation and mediation gained wider informal publicity and support amongst the general community. However, some volunteers reported that whilst, in theory, they intervened as 'ordinary members of the community', this was not the way they were viewed. Volunteers stated that victims and accused usually regarded them as representatives of the police, fiscal service or social work department. Volunteers would generally not reveal their voluntary role unless specifically asked.

The interviewees suggested that volunteers might not be as reliable as paid staff in terms of maintaining a consistent and fairly high case load. They might also be more likely to leave the project, with the result that the training input would be wasted.

The costs involved in the use of trained volunteer mediators are discussed in detail in Chapter Eight. The study of the costs of reparation and mediation included the costs of recruiting, training, supervising and supporting volunteers. To operate the scheme using volunteers it was essential that a paid member of staff be available to deal with these issues and to liaise with other agencies, notably fiscals.

The overall cost per case of reparation and mediation was higher in Edinburgh than Glasgow. This was partly because the scheme in Edinburgh operated under-capacity thus increasing the cost per case. Knapp and Netten suggest that whilst there were few cost advantages of using volunteers this could be transitory as the scheme took on more cases.

Summary

In Edinburgh volunteers were trained as mediators. The scheme had been able to attract sufficient experienced and committed volunteers to operate successfully. There appeared to be no particular benefits or drawbacks, including in cost terms, of using volunteers rather than paid staff.

8 Reparation, mediation and prosecution: Comparative costs

Martin Knapp and Ann Netten

The pursuit of cost information

The White Paper, *Crime, Justice and Protecting the Public* (HMSO, 1990), though not directly applicable to Scotland, nevertheless helps to set the present context for this study, as well as the broad policy philosophy within which diversion schemes operate. Probably more than any previous policy statement in recent years, the 1990 White Paper placed great emphasis on the expenditure implications of sentencing options. It reported expected total annual expenditure on criminal justice services of £7 billion in 1990, an increase of 77 per cent in real terms since 1980. While the role of comparative costs in sentencing options must necessarily be limited, the White Paper proposes legislation that would:

> place a new duty on the Secretary of State to inform the courts annually of the costs of implementing penalties and to publish information about the costs of the criminal justice system for the attention of those who take decisions in the system. (para 2.21)

The aim was to increase awareness of the implications of decisions made at each stage of the criminal justice system. Although the rationale for an increased emphasis on punishment in the community was to achieve more appropriate and effective sentencing, it was acknowledged that a reduction of the burden on the taxpayer was also desirable (para 9.3).

One obvious corollary is that innovative methods of dealing with offences or offenders need to demonstrate not only that they can be effective in achieving their rehabilitation, punishment or retribution aims, but that their resource implications are properly appreciated. Whether one likes it or not, wider acceptance of innovations within the criminal justice system will often depend in part on their resource implications.

This chapter is concerned with the resource or cost implications of the two SACRO reparation and mediation schemes and of prosecution. It describes the costing methodology; it examines in detail the activities undertaken and the costs associated with each; and it reports the comprehensive and similarly disaggregated costs of prosecution. First, the context within which the cost findings should be considered is briefly described.

The practice context of researching costs

Public policy decisions cannot sensibly be undertaken in a cost vacuum. For any organisation funding and management of innovations as well as long-standing services each require an appreciation of the financial implications of alternative courses of action. This does not mean that the criterion of relative cost-effectiveness (or worse, the criterion of cheapness) must necessarily be adopted. Especially with newly established services, or those developing new roles within an evolving system of provision or decision-making, a narrow interpretation of cost-effectiveness can be very misleading. This is an important consideration in the present context. The two reparation and mediation schemes were not established simply to replace or substitute for prosecution, but partly to act as supplements to them. Moreover, the schemes were seeking to set up new service arrangements within their areas (and examining the contributions of volunteers in one case) so that they, and the agencies with which they were working, were likely to be starting a little way down their respective learning curves.

These circumstances had some bearing on the research design, and should also be borne in mind in the interpretation of the cost findings. Of the many consequences of such a context for the present study, two are of particular salience. First, comparisons have been made between the costs of reparation and mediation and prosecution but we would not want this to encourage the view that the two are strict alternatives. The reparation and mediation schemes were not purely diversion services, for their attempts to take accused persons out of the criminal justice system represent just one of a number of aims. As a supplement or adjunct to prosecution their justification was not and should not be that they will save money. It would therefore be inappropriate to employ a narrow cost-effectiveness criterion or to overplay its relevance. Secondly, what was costed was what was in place, not what might have been. We have not engaged in much cost futurology. The small scale of the schemes, the spare capacity in one of them (beyond the effective control of the scheme), the types of accused or offence with which they were dealing, the funding uncertainties, and the point during the prosecution process at which reparation and mediation became an option were all pre-determined characteristics of reparation and mediation, beyond the control of SACRO yet quite likely to influence their costs. In the final section of this chapter we will therefore make some conjectures about the costs of reparation and mediation were it to be serving a different clientele or operating in different ways, but until then we concentrate on the services as provided in the context which pertained during 1989-90; that is, we costed *what was* and not what ought to be.

Methodology

In this costs study we have adhered as closely as possible to well-established costing procedures developed in previous research, especially in public or social policy contexts, including criminal justice studies. These procedures reduce to four broad costing rules. Compliance with these rules increases the likelihood of a valid evidence base for policy debate. These four rules are described in more detail, and illustrated in a variety of social care applications, in Knapp (1990). They have been used in other criminal justice contexts, including evaluations of community service in Scotland (Knapp et al, 1990), of prisons (Knapp and Fenyo, 1988; forthcoming), and of intermediate treatment (Knapp et al, 1992). Because the discipline of the market has limited relevance in determining the supply of most criminal justice services, the supply price, which is otherwise assumed to be linked to the full cost of production, cannot be relied upon to indicate the true economic or social value of the services delivered. The costing rules are designed in part to correct for the distortions which flow from removal from the market, and to reflect the multiple funding and provision of the criminal justice system. They also emphasise the need for careful comparisons and the integration of cost information with outcome findings.

Basic costing rules

The first costing rule is to define costs comprehensively to include all resource impacts of the policies, practices or decisions under study, wheresoever they may fall. There should be consistently comprehensive cost definitions for the different options. For example, some of the resource implications of prosecution fell outside the budgets of the procurators fiscal and the courts and would need to be included.

The second rule follows from the realisation that costs will not be identical for every reparation and mediation case, nor for every person prosecuted through the courts. Some differences will be attributable to individual circumstances and alleged offences; for example, some may stem from the use of volunteers in Edinburgh but not in Glasgow. The second rule is to recognise and explore (in so far as data allow) the reasons for cost variations.

The immediate corollary and third costing rule is to make only like-with-like comparisons. Inter-personal differences in costs are likely to be systematically associated with the alternative routes taken by cases after they had been marked by fiscals. The decision to prosecute is not random so that the costs of prosecution and reparation and mediation may differ because of the different clienteles they serve. Cost studies should compare like with like.

The fourth and final costing rule is an extension of the third: cost results should be set alongside or integrated with evidence on outcomes. Costs are simply the summary measures of the resources employed in dealing with, and perhaps prosecuting, those accused of offences, and those resources have been brought together in the hope of having some desirable effects on the accused, the victims and society. Costs are but one element in a larger system, and it would be foolish to disregard other parts of the system in an evaluation.

Pricing services and resources

In aggregating resources employed to arrive at a measure of cost we need to attach monetary values (prices or shadow prices). Economic theory urges us to attach prices which reflect opportunity costs. The opportunity costing approach recognises that the quoted price of a resource or service may not reflect its true social value. In particular, some inputs may have no market price at all. An example would be volunteer inputs into the Edinburgh reparation scheme. The preferred measure of price is the long-run marginal cost (LRMC), usually approximated with sufficient accuracy by the short-run average cost. Costs are expressed in 1989-90 prices.

The comparative design

The two reparation and mediation schemes were, as we have seen, only partly to be seen as alternatives to prosecution. A key methodological assumption is that the appropriate costs to examine are those which *additionally* arose in the reparation and mediation stream. In particular, cases which were referred to reparation and mediation but which failed (for whatever reason) are assumed to return to the fiscal for re-marking, and thereafter the costs are assumed to be the same as would have arisen had they not been marked for reparation in the first place. The cases which started out on the reparation and mediation path but failed to complete must be costed. In these cases there was a temporary diversion from the prosecution stream which resulted in costs for SACRO and for the fiscals who had to deal with a case twice. Everything else remained equal. There was one exception to this, when a reparation and mediation case was breached after the initial agreement had been drawn up between accused and victim, and where the reason for the breach was in some way an outcome of the process of reparation and mediation itself. In these circumstances it would be appropriate to include the costs of any sentence arising from the breach in the costs of reparation and mediation. Because it was not known how many agreements were breached in these circumstances such costs could not be attached in this study. For some policy discussions it is appropriate to add the costs of failed reparation and mediation cases in to the costs of successful cases. We return to this point later.

It should be noted that this design and arrangement of the costs findings produces exactly the same results as a comparison of, say 100 prosecution cases and 100 reparation and mediation cases from beginning to end (including failed reparation and mediation which resulted in prosecution). A little algebra will confirm that this is so.

Bottom up and top down

There is one major difference between the costing approaches employed for reparation and mediation and for prosecution: for the former we work from the *top down*, taking the annual SACRO accounts, supplementing them with relevant information, and then allocating every last penny to activities; for the latter we use a *bottom up* approach, listing, quantifying and costing the various elements that go to define prosecution. If performed correctly on the same service, the two approaches would produce identical results. The bottom up approach is more susceptible to errors of omission. If some services or activities had been missed the resultant prosecution cost would be an underestimate of the true cost.

The costs of reparation and mediation

The aims of the SACRO schemes included an emphasis on two of the central themes in criminal justice policy discussions today: recognition of the needs of victims, and working with accused to bring home to them the implications of their actions. One important task in the costing, therefore, was to recognise that reparation and mediation work went on with both accused and victims. The schemes ran through a well-defined sequence of activities:

* referral by the fiscal;

* case vetted by the project worker and perhaps discussed with the fiscal;

* victim contacted and views discovered about participation in reparation and mediation;

* accused contacted and views discovered about participation in reparation and mediation;

* agreement drawn up between victim and accused;

* agreement implemented;

* agreement breached in a small number of cases, case returned to the fiscal;

* agreement completed according to plan and the fiscal informed;

* payment of compensation money (if any) by SACRO to victim or charity.

Cases came to the projects from Edinburgh District Court and Glasgow District and Stipendiary Magistrate Court (the Glasgow project served the whole of the city). Glasgow's District Court dealt with offences of a seriousness which would go to the Sheriff Court elsewhere in Scotland. The intention was that some cases would have been diverted from Edinburgh Sheriff Court but an analysis of the outcomes of cases which were returned from the project during the monitoring period revealed that with only one exception cases were routed to the District Court. Reparation and mediation tended to deal with relatively minor cases which, if prosecuted, would be more likely to get a non-custodial sentence than any other, but trivial offences would not be taken up, since they would not have been prosecuted. There needed to be sufficient evidence of an offence being committed before a case was referred to either of the projects.

In costing reparation and mediation we first obtained the audited accounts for the year ended 31 March 1990, and made adjustments to ensure consistency of inclusion and exclusion of different expenditure heads, bearing in mind what would be available for the prosecution stream. This gave the total direct costs. Secondly, using information on how staff allocated their time across a number of specified activities the total direct costs were allocated across component activities. Thirdly, by weighting these direct component costs by measures of workload (such as the number of referrals and agreements), average direct costs were obtained. The fourth stage was to estimate the indirect costs of reparation and mediation falling on other agencies or individuals. In fact, these were negligible for the majority of cases, though we discuss later the implications for the fiscals and others in the event of failure or breach. Stages two to four above work with the component activities of reparation and mediation. The final stage, therefore, was to calculate the full cost of reparation and mediation.

In the table 8.1 (below) expenditure by activity has not been apportioned nor has scale been adjusted for (to get average costs).

Direct cost calculations

The reparation and mediation accounts were consolidated and managed from the Edinburgh office, but interviews with staff made it possible to apportion costs between the projects, as detailed in Table 8.1.

Reparation and mediation is obviously labour-intensive, with two-thirds of total direct expenditure allocated to staff. Direct capital cost estimates are excluded, though a rent and rates element is included. It was not possible to estimate the opportunity costs of capital associated with the buildings used by SACRO in delivering reparation and mediation. Whilst the use of rent and rates is sub-optimal, we do not believe that this underestimates the full cost, nor distorts either the comparisons between projects, or between reparation and mediation and prosecution.

Table 8.1
The total costs of reparation and mediation 1989-90

Item of Expenditure	Edinburgh £	Glasgow £	Total £
Salaries, NI, superannuation(1)	25333	25333	50665
Rent, rates, insurance, repairs	3441	3441	6882
Printing, stationery	1758	1758	3516
Heat, light and cleaning	174	174	348
Travel expenses (2)	1690	4207	5897
Telephone	782	782	1564
Petty cash	0	760	760
Postage	113	113	225
Publications, conference fees, subs	137	137	274
Miscellaneous	745	745	1489
Volunteer expenses (3)	1691	0	1691
Bank interest	76	76	151
Total	35940	37526	73461

(1) The project manager's costs and some of the Edinburgh administrator's costs were allocated equally to the two schemes. Edinburgh had, in addition, a volunteer coordinator and a part-time administrator. Glasgow had a project worker and part-time administrator. Since March 1990 staffing arrangements have changed somewhat. SACRO National Office costs; overhead administration, fund-raising and so on, have not been included. The equivalent elements for the prosecution stream are not costed either.

(2) The Glasgow mode of working necessarily involved a lot of travelling by the project worker. Volunteers' travelling costs are included in volunteer expenses below.

(3) Includes travel and subsistence, plus other out-of-pocket expenses (such as costs of child-minding for single parent volunteers).

Apportioning the direct costs of reparation and mediation by activity

Following discussions with SACRO staff, six component activities of reparation and mediation were distinguished:

* development work, including establishing project, publicity and public relations;

* dealing with referrals from the fiscals, some of which were not accepted as suitable;

* working towards agreements between victim and accused;

* processing agreements;

* dealing with breaches;

* dealing with successfully completed agreements, including notifying the fiscals and paying compensation monies.

In Edinburgh SACRO staff also trained and supported volunteers, though this activity is hard to separate from the third and fourth activities, and in the time and expenditure allocations, the work with volunteers is not distinguished.

In interviews we examined the allocation of staff time between activities, concentrating on the year ended 31 March 1990. Staff arrangements have subsequently altered. General project management time was automatically allocated *pro rata* across the other six activities when the interviews were conducted. Developmental work was not included when attributing costs to current cases, and because the two schemes were in their early days there was still a lot of this work.

Staff time allocations are reported in Table 8.2. These apportionments, together with assumptions about the allocation of associated non-staff resources, allow us to calculate the total cost or expenditure for each activity for 1989-90. Differences between schemes emerged but will be considered after calculation of average and indirect costs.

Table 8.2
Staff time allocations, total expenditures and average direct costs by activity
(Costs are expressed in pounds sterling at 1989-90 prices)

Activity	Staff Time(1)		Total Cost(2)		Workload(3)		Average Cost(4)	
	E	G	E	G	E	G	E	G
	%	%	£	£	%	%	£	£
Development work(5)	18	15	6469	5629	-	-	-	-
Referrals	12	10	4087	3432	176	272	23	13
Working towards agreements	57	58	20903	21925	161	230	130	95
Processing agreements	10	12	3598	4624	88	135	41	34
Dealing with breaches	1	1	175	433	10	14	18	31
Closing a successful case	2	4	708	1483	78	121	9	12
Total	100	100	35940	37526	-	-	-	-

E = Edinburgh, G = Glasgow

(1) Allocations are for project worker or volunteer coordinator and administrator combined in each of the two schemes, with project management and project administration time allocated *pro rata*.
(2) Calculated from staff time allocations and assumptions about the allocation of non-staff expenditures.
(3) From SACRO records, with estimates for numbers of referrals taken from Chapter Two. Numbers refer to cases.
(4) Total cost divided by workload.
(5) The associated costs of development work are taken out and not allocated to current clients. These resources were expended to help establish the new service in the two areas.

The average direct costs of reparation and mediation

For each activity, with the exception of referrals, we obtained a workload/output measure from the two schemes, relying on data already gathered by SACRO. For referrals we used the data gathered during the five month monitoring period. On average, each 100 accepted cases in Edinburgh produced 9 rejections by reparation and mediation, and in Glasgow there were 18 rejected cases per 100 acceptances. Applying multipliers calculated from this sample period to the full year (161 accepted cases in Edinburgh, 230 in Glasgow) we estimated the referral figures for the year.

The workload data corresponded exactly to the financial year 1989-90. Edinburgh dealt with fewer cases than Glasgow at each stage, as Table 8.2 shows. Agreements started during the year and completed (successfully or in breach) after 31 March, and referrals in the previous year which carried over into this, caused only minor difficulties. The numbers of completions during the financial year are taken as the appropriate workload measures. Cross-year flows or hangovers will not distort the picture much, even with a rapidly expanding or contracting service, since the modal length of time between referral and completion is of the order of only 4 to 6 weeks. In Edinburgh, there were 78 successful completions in 1989-90 and 10 breaches. In Glasgow, the figures were 121 and 14 respectively. These sum exactly to the number of agreements drawn up during the year, indicating no problem with hangovers unless breach probabilities had altered. SACRO staff did not believe that this was the case.

Although SACRO played some part in the process of acceptance or rejection of cases, the scale of activity was essentially exogenously determined. In Edinburgh staff believed that they could deal with more cases within current resources. The Glasgow scheme had reached full capacity, which may partly account for the difference in rejection rates.

Dividing total cost for each activity by workload gives the component average direct costs of reparation and mediation activities (see the final two columns of Table 8.2 above). With the exception of closing a successful case and dealing with breaches, component average direct costs were higher in Edinburgh than in Glasgow. By breaking down the costs associated with the various activities in this way, it is possible to observe and cost the fixed and variable elements of reparation and mediation, to cost cases which reached different stages within the full process from referral to completion, and to repackage the costs under varying assumptions about the expansion of reparation and mediation to other types of case or circumstance.

The indirect costs of reparation and mediation

There were few indirect costs for reparation and mediation cases. Some clients were receiving social work support, income maintenance, subsidised housing, counselling for alcohol-related problems, and so on, but in the majority of cases receipt of these services was quite independent of reparation and mediation and would have been received had the accused been prosecuted. In the small number of cases which took the prosecution channel and which resulted in a custodial sentence, some of these services, such as social work support, would have (temporarily) ceased, and the cost savings that would result should be offset against the costs of custody. This is likely to be such a rare occurrence in the present context (see Chapter Four) that no such adjustment has been made. In this study, evaluating differences between the two SACRO schemes, and between them and prosecution (and perhaps some other forms of diversion), it is only necessary to cost those services or inputs which would not have been supplied in every alternative, holding constant the characteristics of individual cases.

The SACRO projects did not provide social work support, and clients of reparation and mediation who were thought to need previously unsupplied social work services were directed towards a social work diversion programme where available. In contrast, some alcohol or marriage guidance counselling or psychiatric services were initiated (but not delivered) by the SACRO projects. During 1989-90, 30 out of 391 accepted referrals across the two projects (8 per cent) were referred on to other agencies. Averaging these counselling and psychiatric service costs across all accepted referrals and assuming a mean unit cost of £50 for each new case gives additional indirect costs of £3.84 per case. The assumption here is that some of the cases referred on for psychiatric, marriage guidance or alcohol counselling would go no further than an initial appointment, and others would attend a series of counselling sessions. The cost is based on work done elsewhere by the authors with the (former) National Marriage Guidance Council and the study of a variety of psychiatric services.

The SACRO overheads to the projects (central office, fund-raising, and so on) were not costed. For example, the Director of SACRO had line management and project development responsibilities which amounted to about one day every three weeks; and there were SACRO project development costs. There were parallel activities and associated costs for prosecution which were also not costed. These were the supervision and general management time of senior fiscal staff, and indeed the costs of tax collection to fund prosecution.

Although the time inputs of senior SACRO or fiscal staff were not costed there were inputs into reparation and mediation from the fiscal staff at the initial marking stage. Marking cases for diversion to reparation and mediation was argued to be more time consuming than marking for prosecution, though in interviews fiscals also noted that this short term burden was worth the long term benefits. Cases may also have to be referred back to senior fiscals (perhaps on numerous occasions) once there has been a response from the victim and accused, when an agreement has been reached and at successful completion.

The fiscal's work with failed cases (including breached agreements) which go back into the prosecution stream was not costed within the methodology employed here, for this would have happened anyway if the case had been prosecuted in the first place. The omission of these costs is possible because of the way failure costs have been added back into the costs of success. The other fiscal costs are included, that is the work falling on senior fiscals (assistant fiscals in Glasgow, senior deputes in Edinburgh), amounting in some cases to more than half a day a week. From detailed data collected by the Crown Office, the cost of marking for diversion averages £3.08 per case, to which we added the estimated costs (in the absence of any data) of £5 per case for other fiscal inputs to each of the three stages of drawing up agreements, processing them and wrapping up successful completions.

The Edinburgh scheme made extensive use of volunteers. The costs of recruitment, training and ongoing supervision and support were included and allocated across the component activities of reparation and mediation. These were higher than might be found elsewhere because of the scale of the scheme. A much larger reparation and mediation volunteer-mediator scheme would need little additional training overheads. It was pointed out during one of the interviews that the fiscals would be unable to make direct use of volunteers, partly because it was believed that people were more willing to volunteer when a service was under the auspices of a voluntary rather than a statutory agency, and partly because recruiting, training and supervising volunteers was time-consuming. The costs of employing the volunteer co-ordinator and project manager were effectively the costs of having volunteers.

The direct, out-of-pocket costs to the volunteers themselves have also been included in the accounts in so far as they are claimed (see Table 8.1), but are there hidden costs which have so far been missed? These hidden costs would be the opportunity costs to the volunteers or to society of these people working on reparation and mediation and not on something else. If, for example, a volunteer had given up work in order to contribute to the Edinburgh reparation and mediation scheme, what earnings were sacrificed, and what associated productivity was lost to the UK economy?

These are important issues to address, not simply because we wish to compute the full social costs of reparation and mediation and its alternatives, but also because the expansion of a volunteer reparation and mediation scheme, or the establishment of such projects elsewhere in the country, might not be able to recruit the same number or calibre of volunteers and would therefore face direct rather than hidden costs of finding and employing suitable staff. In the event, we considered it unnecessary to attach a cost. SACRO had experienced no difficulty in recruiting volunteers. There appeared, therefore, to be no supply constraint. Many volunteers had skills directly relevant to reparation and mediation, such as a retired ACAS employee, which might not have been available if paid staff had been sought. It was found that the volunteers were not giving up anything for which they were not compensated in the short term through SACRO expenses. Neither, it appeared, had they given up other volunteering activities to work on reparation and mediation. Indeed, as the previous chapter shows some volunteers had gained much from their activities. No value was put on these volunteer benefits.

Table 8.3
Direct, indirect and aggregate average costs of reparation and mediation, by activity in pounds

Activity	Direct Cost		Indirect Cost		Aggregate Cost	
	E	G	E	G	E	G
	£	£	£	£	£	£
Referrals	23	13	3	3	26	16
Working towards agreements	130	95	9	9	139	104
Processing agreements	41	34	5	5	46	39
Dealing with breaches	18	31	0	0	18	31
Closing a successful case	9	12	9	12	9	12

E = Edinburgh, G = Glasgow

In summary, the indirect costs of reparation and mediation were the costs of counselling (marriage guidance, alcohol, psychiatric) added to each case with which SACRO was working to reach an agreement; the cost of marking cases for reparation and mediation (added to each referral) and other the fiscal inputs to various stages. These pushed up the average costs for the component activities as shown in Table 8.3. above.

It is not necessary to add a cost for offending during the reparation and mediation period. Interviews revealed that it was almost inconceivable that further offences would be committed during this period. SACRO staff could not recall a single incident; every breach of an agreement was a consequence of failure to keep the agreement and not re-offending. This is not surprising, since most reparation and mediation clients were first-time accused who had elected to take the reparation and mediation channel to avoid criminalisation. As one SACRO interviewee commented: 'most of them didn't go out offending; they just went out and something happened to them'. Re-offending would not be likely. Other reparation and mediation clients, those with a criminal record, were no more likely to re-offend during reparation and mediation than if prosecuted; indeed, SACRO staff were of the view that subsequent re-offending propensities would be lower for reparation and mediation clients. Any additional costs for re-offending do not therefore need to be included.

The full costs of reparation and mediation

The costs of reparation and mediation varied because of differences in alleged offences, client characteristics, and the stage reached in the reparation and mediation process. Neighbourhood disputes and relationship cases (between victim and accused) could be complex and therefore costly because of disputes over what actually happened, but this same complexity made these cases expensive to prosecute through court. Generally, it was not the type of offence but the type of agreement that determined the time taken and the cost. In this study it was not possible to disaggregate costs by type of offence or type of agreement, although they can be disaggregated by stage reached. These are shown in Table 8.4.

The full, direct plus indirect costs of reparation and mediation can be calculated for four different case types:

* Cases marked and referred by the fiscal but not accepted by SACRO, thence referred back to the fiscal. For the 15 Edinburgh and 42 Glasgow cases, the total cost was the cost of referral (direct SACRO costs and costs of marking by the fiscals).

Table 8.4
The full costs of reparation and mediation by type of case, and the effective cost per successful completion

Type of Case	Edinburgh £	Glasgow £
Marked for reparation and mediation by fiscal but not accepted by SACRO	26[1]	16[1]
Referral accepted, but agreement not drawn up	165[1]	120[1]
Agreement drawn up, but breached before completion	229[1]	190[1]
Successful completion of agreement, case closed	215	176
Effective cost per successful completion, allocating all SACRO and indirect costs to successes	404[2]	298[2]

(1) Most cases returned to the prosecution channel, incurring further costs, though we argue in the text that it would be inappropriate to allocate these prosecution costs to reparation and mediation itself.

(2) The costs of failed cases have been reallocated to successful cases.

* Cases where agreement was not reached between victim and accused because of unwillingness or inability on the part of either party, hence referred back to the fiscal. Agreements were not made in 43 per cent of accepted cases. The cost was the referral and working towards an agreement, amounting to £165 in Edinburgh and £120 in Glasgow.

* Cases which failed at the reparation stage when agreement was not kept. Eleven per cent of agreements were breached (24 out of 223). Many breaches took the form of the accused failing to pay the financial compensation agreed. If reparation and mediation broke down because of the intractability of the victim after an agreement had been drawn up, this was not treated as failure and prosecution would not result. In a small number of those cases where the accused had broken the

agreement the fiscals decided not to proceed with a prosecution. This might occur, for example, when some but not all of a financial compensation agreement had been paid. In other cases, the delays involved through diversion and then within the fiscal office left some cases time-barred. Cost is the cumulative sum of the different stages. For example, in Glasgow the calculation would be as follows for the average breach case: cost of referral (£16) + cost of working towards an agreement (£104) + cost of processing agreement (£39) + cost of dealing with breach (£31). This amounts to £190.

* Cases which proceeded to successful completion of the agreement (78 in Edinburgh and 121 in Glasgow). Costs are cumulative sums: £215 in Edinburgh and £176 in Glasgow.

For the first, second and third groups of cases, the amounts reported in Table 8.4 indicate the additional costs of their temporary diversion away from prosecution. These amounts can be reallocated in one of two ways. They can be attributed to the costs of prosecution itself, under the assumption that it was worth a try by the fiscals to reduce the burden on the courts and to avoid 'criminalisation' of first offenders, but this failed. The costs of the time spent with SACRO are therefore spread across all prosecution cases in the two areas. The inflationary effect on the full population of prosecution cases would be tiny. The other way to attribute these failure costs is to see them as part of the cost of success. Each of the 78 successful cases in Edinburgh came about in the context of 98 other cases marked for reparation and mediation and not reaching successful completion. This latter argument would be marginally preferred if one took the view that these costs would not have arisen if there had been no SACRO project in the first place, and therefore it is sensible to attribute these costs to SACRO. This gives us the effective cost per successful completion of £404 in Edinburgh and £298 in Glasgow. Here, as with other cost calculations, the principal reason for the difference between the two schemes was the unused capacity in the Edinburgh scheme. It was referred fewer cases than it could deal with, compared to the Glasgow scheme which was working at full stretch.

The costs of prosecution

The process of prosecution

Emphasis has already been laid upon the need to compare like with like in estimating cost implications. In describing the process of prosecution, therefore, no attempt was made to encompass the whole of the Scottish prosecution service; the aim was simply to identify the probable paths through the process that would have been taken by a case referred to reparation and mediation.

To recap from Chapter One, with few exceptions, all criminal proceedings in Scotland are instituted by the office of the fiscal, who is responsible for both the investigation and prosecution of crime, although in practice the initial investigation is done by the police. Unless the crime is serious the fiscal will first learn of the crime in the form of a report from the police. It is the fiscal's decision whether or not a case is prosecuted.

Figure 2 (on page 12) illustrates the possible paths through the prosecution process taken by the type of case dealt with by the reparation and mediation project. There has been increased emphasis recently on preventing cases from reaching the courts; during 1989 only 56 per cent of cases reported by the police were prosecuted. This has primarily been due to a rise in the use of conditional offers and fiscal fines. The latter were introduced in 1988, and the annual number of conditional offers has more than doubled since 1985. At present, diversions such as referral to social work represent less than one per cent of all cases that are not prosecuted. A central feature of the SACRO schemes was that they should pick up cases that otherwise would have been prosecuted. Thus the decision not to prosecute, to send a warning letter only, to make a conditional offer (usually a fine) or a fiscal fine (a fixed penalty) were not originally intended to have been options for cases referred to the project. In practice, however, it was found that the reparation and mediation project filled a gap in the criminal justice system. Chapter Four shows the paths taken by the comparison group, demonstrating that other options, such as a warning letter, might have been considered as an alternative to the possibly damaging effects of bringing a prosecution.

Once it has been decided to prosecute, the case is allocated to a court. More serious cases are classified as solemn and require a jury. None of the cases that would be considered for reparation and mediation would be of this nature. Chapter Two describes the types of offence of which reparation and mediation referrals were accused. Generally, more serious cases are dealt with by sheriff courts, and less serious cases by the district courts. In Glasgow, where the pressure on the courts is high, all the cases referred to the reparation and mediation scheme would have been dealt with by the District Court. In Edinburgh, although most cases would have been allocated to the District Court, a few cases may have been allocated to the Sheriff Court, but they would still be relatively minor offences.

After allocation to a district court, a date is fixed for the initial pleading diet in the court and the complaint served upon the accused. The complaint is normally sent by registered post for this type of case, but if this fails it is served by the police. Once the complaint is served the accused must plea either by letter or at the pleading diet. If no plea is made the fiscal will ask for a continuation without plea and set another date for the plea to be heard. If, after repeated attempts to obtain a plea, none is forthcoming a non-appearance warrant may be issued. This is served by the police and can involve holding the accused in custody overnight, although in the type of case being considered here it is more likely that the accused would be required to appear at a police station the following morning and be taken from there to court.

If the plea is guilty the case is disposed of immediately; otherwise a date is set for a trial diet. Most of the preparation of the case for prosecution has been accomplished by the reporting police officer before the report is submitted to the fiscal. This report constitutes a summary of the case and the statements obtained from witnesses. If a plea of not guilty is made by the accused the fiscals' department writes to the police requesting the full statements and any other evidence necessary. Often the defence lawyer will also get in contact with the police officer responsible for the report to discuss the details of the case as the lawyer does not have direct access to the detailed statements by the witnesses.

At or shortly before the trial diet the accused may plead guilty and the case will be disposed of without trial. This can result in a great deal of wasted time and effort in preparation by the police and the fiscal. It has been suggested that late changes of plea are the result of the attitude of the accused and entitlement to legal aid (National Audit Office, 1989). Even if the accused pleads not guilty the trial may not be heard on the date set. Cases are adjourned to a later date because witnesses are not present, for example.

Table 8.5
Disposals by type of offence, Edinburgh and Glasgow District Courts, 1988

Disposal	Minor theft	Fraud	Vanda-lism/ Mal. Mischief	Petty Assault	Breach of Peace	Total
Acquittal/ discharge	167	27	110	378	609	1291 (11%)
Fine	1315	298	758	1406	4187	8064 (70%)
Admonish-ment	185	27	69	225	811	1316 (11%)
Prison(1)	234	20	42	156	324	776 (7%)
Compensation order	10	10	37	1	1	58 (1%)
Other(2)	25	2	14	17	25	83 (O%)
Total	1936	384	1029	2283	5956	11588 (100%)

(1) Includes detention centres and young offenders' institutions
(2) Includes probation, community service orders, 'unfit to plead' etc

Once a plea of guilty has been made or the verdict given the case will be disposed of. Table 8.5 shows the distribution of disposals in district courts in 1988 across the types of case with which the projects were concerned.

It should be noted that one case can result in more than one disposal although only the main penalty is shown in this table. For example, it is possible to impose both a fine and a compensation order and one case may consist of a number of different offences and individuals. The variation with respect to type of offence was limited. Minor theft was more likely to result in imprisonment, and breach of the peace slightly more likely to result in an admonition than other cases. However, the most likely disposal for all offences is the imposition of a fine. In Chapter Four the comparison group is described in detail. This was limited to 44 cases, of which 19 were not prosecuted. Results of disposals were only available for 20 cases. The majority (14) were punished with a fine, with the remaining cases receiving deferred sentences or admonitions. Conclusions from such limited information must necessarily be cautious, but it does seem clear that the most costly disposal, imprisonment, was only likely to result from fine defaulting.

In estimating the costs of prosecution it is important to be clear that what is required is an estimate of the costs that would have been incurred by the type of cases dealt with by the projects and an indication of the implications for costs of extension of the projects. Thus as only one case returned from the reparation and mediation schemes was heard at a sheriff court so a typical costing can be gained by estimating the costs of district court cases. However, in discussing possible extensions of the project, the likelihood of higher costs of cases heard in a sheriff courts (and thus higher potential savings) needs to be taken into consideration. This is discussed at the end of this chapter.

Accounts

Very little information is publicly available in the form of accounts. The Crown Prosecution Service in England currently produces an annual report, but at present there is no comparable report on prosecution in Scotland. Supply Estimates produced by the Treasury for the year's expected expenditure are available, but the categories of expenditure are so broad that they provide little guidance to the likely costs of the administration of prosecution of summary cases.

Costs to procurators fiscal

A global figure was provided by the Crown Office for expenditure of £20,281,000 by the fiscal service as a whole during 1989-90. This includes all salaries and national insurance contributions but excludes capital costs. As Figure 2 suggests, the administrative and court costs will vary considerably depending upon the type of case and the plea made. Bearing in mind the need to identify comparable cases, any attempt simply to divide overall expenditure by the number of cases is far too simplistic.

In estimating the costs to the fiscal, therefore, use was made of the results of a work measurement exercise undertaken during 1990-91 by the Crown Office and the Treasury. The study was intended to provide the

Crown Office with information on the numbers and grades of staff required by the fiscal service and involved the tagging of all cases received during one month and the logging of legal and administrative time spent on each of these cases as they passed through the system (HM Treasury, 1990). Results from over 7,000 cases in fourteen fiscal offices resulted in detailed estimates of time committed for cases that followed different paths through the prosecution process.[1]

Once the fiscal has made the decision to prosecute, the complaint to be served on the accused is prepared and the case allocated to court. A date is arranged for the pleading diet. The work measurement exercise found that administrative officers (AOs) and administrative assistants (AAs) took about a quarter of an hour per case to accomplish this. A further six minutes is spent by a legally trained officer. Here it is assumed that a senior legal assistant would be involved rather than a legal assistant, as the decision between prosecution and non-prosecution is likely to be a fine one in these cases. It was estimated that about 15 minutes is spent on typing the complaint and associated papers, checking, photocopying and so on (MacFarlane, 1990, personal communication).

When the case is brought to court the legal representation of the fiscal consisted of one senior legal assistant who appeared for five minutes on average at a pleading diet. If the case needs to be continued without plea (CWP) additional court time will be involved, so the average length of the pleading diet is assumed to be six minutes. Additional administrative and legal time incurred as a result of a continuation is already accounted for in the timings estimated in the work measurement exercise. If the plea is guilty no further administrative or legal time would be required. If, however, the plea is not guilty then the case would need to be prepared for prosecution. Much of the work at this stage is concerned with contacting the police and requesting statements and dealing with queries. Separate estimates have been made of the preparation costs involved in those cases that plead guilty and those that plead not guilty at the trial diet. Not surprisingly, perhaps, more administrative time is involved in those that plead guilty at the trial diet than those that plead not guilty. Cases that change their pleas between the pleading and trial diets may be involved in a series of negotiations and discussions that can result in more than one change of plea during this period. In some cases the plea will have been received well before the trial diet, in others not until the day. Sometimes executive officers (EOs) become involved in the problems that arise and the assumption has been made that the time is distributed 10 per cent to executive officers, 50 per cent to administrative officers and 40 per

[1]Details are available from Martin Knapp and Ann Netten

cent to administrative assistants.

If the accused pleads guilty at the trial diet, less time is spent on average in legal preparation than if there is a not guilty plea. When the plea is not guilty the case may be adjourned because of non-appearance by witnesses or lack of court time and virtually all the work involved in preparing the case for court has to be repeated for the next court appearance. The National Audit Office (1989) found that the expectation was that, of cases called to court for trial, 40 per cent would plead guilty, 40 per cent would be adjourned and only 20 per cent would be heard.

Non-procurator fiscal costs

Much of the fiscal administration tasks in bringing a case to court concern liaison with the police in contacting witnesses and getting the full details of the case assembled. To date there is little detailed information available and these tasks are assumed to take five hours of police time and a further half an hour of typist's time. Police time is also involved if they need to serve the complaint upon the accused which it is assumed occurs in about 10 per cent of cases. Three officers were employed full-time in Lothian over a two-week period serving citations to attend, summonses and cancellations as part of a study of police work associated with courts (P. Lawrence, personal communication). This study found that each document served took about half an hour of police time. Non-appearance warrants also require administration, investigation, apprehension and holding at a police station. There is no detailed information about these and they are assumed to take about five hours of police time. In the absence of any detailed information it is assumed about 5 per cent of cases require the serving of a non-attendance warrant.

Local authorities are responsible for running the district courts and thus bear the majority of the costs of court time. Court costs include salaries, supplies and services and property costs such as heating, cleaning and so on, and are estimated to be £137 per hour. On average a pleading diet lasts about 6 minutes (see above) and a trial diet 50 minutes in a district court.

In Glasgow the District Council expenditure on the eight district courts in 1989-90 was £1,233,000 excluding the costs of central administration overheads. During the same period expenditure on two district courts in Edinburgh was £343,900. Excluding loan charges and debt repayments but including property costs such as rates and administrative overheads, annual expenditure on the administration of the courts is £335,254 in Edinburgh and £1,175,000 in Glasgow. The courts are open five days each week excluding bank holidays and sit for between four and five hours on average, with reduced hours over the Christmas period. Assuming 252 working days per year the administrative cost of court time can be estimated. It has already been identified that the interest here is not on local variations in costs but in reflecting the savings of the reparation and mediation projects to the criminal justice system. Therefore, rather than identify separately the hourly cost of court time in Glasgow and Edinburgh, the hourly court cost is weighted to reflect the proportion of cases dealt with by the reparation and mediation project.

Many of the cases with which the study is concerned are likely to receive legal aid for defence costs. Legal aid pays for advice and assistance given by duty solicitors, advice by way of representation (ABWOR), and meeting the costs of nominated solicitors. It is possible, indeed likely, that those who nominate a solicitor will have received assistance from the duty solicitor in the first instance. It was not possible to identify the probability of receiving or the likely cost of ABWOR in district courts but the average costs of consulting the duty solicitor, follow up duties and average legal aid payments made to nominated solicitors are available. Inflating base figures from the Annual Report of the Scottish Legal Aid Board (1990) provides a 1989-90 estimate of £14 per case for initial advice and £30 for follow-up duties by the duty solicitor. Cases disposed of without trial cost £281 on average in district courts and cases which come to summary trial are similarly estimated at £390. These figures include solicitors and outlays, but excludes counsel as inappropriate to the type of case under consideration.

The probability that a case will get legal aid needs to be taken into account when estimating average costs. Again it is important to compare like with like. On average only about 17 per cent of all cases seen in district courts receive legal aid payments to nominated solicitors, but this includes a large number of motoring offences which are less likely to receive legal aid. Excluding the offences not referred to the reparation and mediation project, the proportion who receive legal aid payments rises to 24 per cent. Moreover, legal aid pays for defence costs in 60 per cent of cases which proceed to trial in the district courts. Eligibility for legal aid is also an issue. In Chapter Two, the characteristics of the accused referred to the scheme are described: 32 per cent were registered as unemployed and only 48 per cent were employed.

In allocating likely legal aid costs it was assumed that on the basis of eligibility, 40 per cent of all cases would have received advice and assistance from the duty solicitor. Forty per cent of those who proceeded to trial would have received follow up advice, that is nine per cent of all cases. Of those going to trial 60 per cent would have their defence by a nominated solicitor paid for by legal aid. This accounts for 13 per cent of all cases. Allowing for a further 14 per cent of those cases not proceeding to trial to receive the help of a nominated solicitor reflects the type of offence that were dealt with by the project.

There are two types of witnesses: professional and non-professional. On average, non-professional witnesses were paid £25 in district courts for expenses and loss of income during 1989-90 (Ewing, 1990). There are usually about four or five witnesses involved in the type of case under consideration. The police serve the citations for these witnesses to attend court and notify the fiscal of the execution of service.

In the minor cases that the reparation and mediation project was concerned with, the only type of professional witnesses likely to be involved would be police officers. The National Audit Office Report (1989) on the fiscal service included some discussion of the waste of police time associated with prosecution (£2.5 million in Scotland as a whole during 1987). This is due primarily to time taken in travelling to and from court and in waiting for cases to be brought before the court. For the purposes of this costing exercise it is assumed that each police officer (there are usually two who appear as witnesses) takes two hours to travel to and wait for a case to be heard. If the accused pleads guilty at this stage no further costs are incurred. A further hour is assumed spent by each officer if the plea is not guilty and the case comes to trial. Additional costs to the police have been identified resulting from short notice given for court appearances which entitle police officers to time off in lieu and/or additional overtime payments (National Audit Office, 1989). Although no specific allowance has been made for these, the estimating procedure does allow for the main reason for this short notice: frequent adjournments of hearings.

Finally, the cost of disposals needs to be established. It was noted earlier that there are few alternative disposals in practice. If the accused was found or pled guilty, the figures in Table 8.5 show the most likely disposal to be a fine. The level of fines imposed will depend on the accused's ability to pay as well as the offence committed. It was decided, therefore, that the most appropriate estimate of the average fine imposed was the average fine per person in the control group: £74. Once a fine has been imposed, an instalment rate (if appropriate) is negotiated, based on the income of the offender, and payments are made usually weekly or fortnightly. Although there is no information about the administrative costs of this process, information is available about the time involved in the administration of fiscal fines from the work measurement exercise.

If offenders do not pay, they will be sent a warning letter by the court. If this does not result in payment, and they have not had the alternative of imprisonment set at imposition, they are required to appear at a means enquiry court (MEC) which may give the offender more time to pay or adjust the level of the instalments. As with the original complaint, citations to attend this court may be served by the police. If the offender does not appear then a non-appearance warrant may be issued. After two appearances at an MEC the offender may be imprisoned immediately for non-payment of fines. A study of fines in Airdrie in 1980-83 found that 65 per cent of persons paid their fines as ordered by the court and 19 per cent paid promptly after receiving the warning letter. Two per cent had their fines remitted or reduced and 10 per cent paid after enforcement procedures of some kind. The imprisonment rate for non-payment at that time was four per cent (Millar, 1984).

In taking into account the costs of administering fines therefore, it is necessary to allow for additional costs associated with enforcement: administration, serving citations to attend, court appearances, non-attendance warrants and prison sentences. A study conducted on a sample of defaulters attending means enquiry courts in 1987 found that 72 per cent of defaulters were unemployed (Nicholson, 1990). Ideally, the influence of such factors on the likelihood of defaulting would be included in the costing of fines, but in the absence of information about the employment status of those who do not default this is not possible. It is possible, however, to incorporate the information about likely payment rates and procedures of enforcement: it is assumed that four per cent of cases default and are imprisoned and that of the remaining cases the same proportion as in the Airdrie study pay immediately, after a warning letter and so on. The average sentence served is 11 days for defaulting on a fine (Nicholson and Millar, 1989, p.74). The average net expenditure per inmate year in Scottish prisons in 1988-89 exclusive of capital was £19,336 (SHHD, 1989). Inflating this to 1989-90 prices gives an average daily cost of £56. Using these assumptions it is estimated that a fine results in a net revenue (or negative cost) of £36.

A compensation order would result in administrative costs to the court without the income resulting from the successful collection of a fine. Compensation was ordered to be paid in only one case in the comparison group and was associated with a fine for the same offence. No additional costs are assumed to be incurred by the imposition of a compensation order. Admonitions were assumed to result in an additional five minutes of court time.

Two of the cases in the comparison group resulted in deferred sentences. There is no information about comparable offences which would give an indication of the likely outcome of a deferred sentence, although, inevitably, a further court appearance would result. In a recent study 43 per cent of deferred sentences required more than one further court appearance. The average number of court appearances per case was 1.65 (Nicholson, 1992). It is reasonable to suppose that each appearance would take about the same length of time as a pleading diet (5 minutes). In the absence of data about likely disposals it is assumed that the same proportion of deferred cases receive fines and admonitions as non-deferred cases. On this basis the net cost of a deferred sentence is a negative cost of £3.

Using these assumptions the net effect of the disposals of the comparison group (described in Chapter Four) was £25 revenue because of the dominant use of fines. Official statistics record the final disposal rather than the use of deferred sentences which precludes any other estimate of the average cost of disposal of this type of case.

Total package costs

The previous section identified the sources of data and the basis upon which the costs of the different stages of the prosecution process can be estimated. It is now possible to estimate the costs of different 'packages' or paths through the prosecution process. Assuming that a case is prosecuted at all, there are three paths that the cases can take:

* If the accused pleads guilty at the *pleading diet*, the costs incurred are those of marking and allocating the case to a court plus the court appearance. This totals £37 if there is no defence and if no legal aid payments are made. This may occur if, for example, the plea is made by letter read out in court. If the full legal aid costs for a non-trial case were accrued, the cost of this path would be £332. The assumptions about the probability of receiving aid and assistance and the legal costs when there was a nominated solicitor which were described above result in an average cost of £74 per case.

* In the event that the accused pleads guilty at the *trial diet*, a trial date will be set and the cost of preparation for the trial (both prosecution and defence) and the cost of the hearing needs to be added to the cost of the pleading diet. In total this package is estimated to cost £322 without legal aid. If legal aid is claimed the cost of this path rises to £756. The assumptions about legal aid result in an average cost of £573.

* In considering the costs of prosecuting a case in which the accused *pleads not guilty,* it is necessary to take into account the effects of adjournments upon cases. Not all the information gathered is related to the number of court appearances associated with the trial, and these

costs must be assumed to be fixed for all cases which come to trial. Thus the cost of the pleading diet, police preparation time and costs incurred serving citations to witnesses, witness payments and the trial diet itself total £469. A postponed hearing is assumed to result in 90 per cent of the fiscal administrative and preparation costs having to be repeated, witnesses served citations to attend the rearranged hearing, five minutes court time and four hours of police time. These assumptions yield an estimated cost of £112 per adjournment. It has been identified that cases have a two-thirds chance of not being heard if they are called to court and retain the plea of guilt (National Audit Office, 1989). Assuming a maximum of six adjournments and the probability of an adjournment remaining the same throughout[1] the additional cost because of adjournments is £206. The total costs of a case coming to trial are thus estimated as £674 excluding legal aid, £1108 when legal aid is claimed and £926 using the above assumptions about receiving legal aid.

Once through the prosecution process, whatever the path, the cost of the disposal needs to be added to the total package. We earlier identified the costs of the elements of the most likely disposals in the event of a guilty finding: a fine, a deferred sentence or an admonition.

Although the original intention was that only cases which otherwise would have been prosecuted would be referred, Chapter Six shows that the reparation and mediation project was perceived by the fiscals as filling a gap in the criminal justice system for certain types of case. Prosecution would have been a likely option in all these cases but it is possible, for example in the case of some neighbourhood disputes, that prosecution would be ineffective or even damaging and a warning letter might have previously been sent. The average cost of this option is estimated as £3. Chapter Four describes the different paths through the criminal justice system taken by the comparison group. The degree to which the comparison group reflects the alternatives that would have been taken in the absence of the reparation and mediation schemes is debatable, but it is notable that 19 of the 44 cases in this group were not prosecuted. The decision not to proceed with a case is estimated to cost the fiscal service £6 on average, in administrative and legal time.

---

[1]To allow for the possibility and associated costs of a larger number of adjourned hearings all the probabilities of more than six adjournments are assumed to accrue to have six adjournments. Thus total adjournment costs = .22(1) + .15(20) + .1(3) + .07(4) + .04(5) + .09(6). Bracketed figures refer to number of adjourned hearings.

The estimates above allow comparison of the costs of reparation and mediation with specific alternative paths through the criminal justice system. At one cost extreme, if the case would not have been prosecuted the case would still have incurred the costs of a warning letter (£3). At the other extreme, a case that came to trial resulting in an admonition would cost an average of £1,119. Such a wide variation in the possible costs of the alternatives to reparation and mediation highlights the need for, and also the dangers of, an estimate of an average cost which takes into account the probabilities of each path through the prosecution process. The information needed is the likelihood that:

* the case would have been prosecuted,

* the accused would plead guilty at the pleading diet,

* the accused would plead guilty at the trial diet.

It is worth noting that many of the accused in the cases with which the project was concerned were likely to have pled guilty as a tacit admission of guilt was required in order for entry on to the project. At what stage the accused would plead guilty in the prosecution process, however, is not at all clear. In 1989 in district courts as a whole, over 78 per cent of cases pled guilty at the pleading diet. Over 12 per cent of cases pled guilty at the trial diet, leaving just over 9 per cent of cases to proceed to a full trial.

One of the distinguishing features of the reparation and mediation project however, was that it did not deal with the average district court case: it specialised in those cases where the victim was identifiable and often known to the accused. In particular it excluded traffic offences. The difference between the average district court case and the cases referred to the reparation and mediation schemes can be illustrated by the fact that of the types of case referred to the schemes 11 per cent were found not guilty or not proven (see Table 8.5), but of all district court cases only about 9 per cent pled not guilty. Even allowing for the high proportion of cases that were not prosecuted in the comparison group the average cost of a comparison group case is estimated as £261. Assuming the same average effect of disposal where individuals were found guilty results in an average cost of £250. If these proportions are applied the average cost is £220 using the assumptions given above about legal aid. Because the net effect of expected disposals is a negative cost or revenue, including the cost of disposal results in an expected cost of £195.

There is no easy way, therefore, of estimating a comparable average cost of the alternative to the reparation and mediation schemes. What we have shown, however, are the costs of the different paths, allowing comparisons of particular types of case.

Discussion

The costs of traditional prosecution and the comparatively new reparation and mediation services introduced by SACRO have been calculated and presented in this chapter. As we illustrated at various stages, attaching costs to these two options means exploring the resource implications of many different routes that can be taken through the options. There are also cost implications for different agencies. How do the costs compare between reparation and mediation and with prosecution?

Edinburgh-Glasgow cost differences

For reparation and mediation the most useful measure of cost is the effective average cost per successful completion, which incorporates the costs of 'failure' within the costs for successful cases. This gives costs of £404 in Edinburgh, and £298 in Glasgow.

The lower cost in Glasgow stems from a number of factors. A significant factor is that, unlike Edinburgh, the Glasgow scheme was operating at its full capacity. We cannot estimate the cost should the Edinburgh scheme reach full caseload capacity, but what the scheme regards as the limited supply of cases from the fiscals has had an important effect. This can be seen in relation to a number of cost elements, including the training and supervision of volunteers. At present, therefore, there are few cost advantages flowing from the use of volunteer mediators, though this would be a transitory phenomenon were the Edinburgh scheme to grow. There is evidence of numerous non-cost benefits from the volunteers, both for reparation and mediation and for the volunteers as individuals.

Cost differences between reparation and mediation and prosecution

We have endeavoured to cost reparation and mediation and prosecution comprehensively and consistently, though omissions have been forced upon us by practicalities. For example, we could not obtain information which allowed calculation of the full opportunity costs of capital. We did not consider it appropriate to attribute costs to the volunteers themselves (though, equally, we did not put monetary values on the benefits of volunteering). We have also not put a cost on the criminalisation of those who proceed through the prosecution channel (the costs which might flow from acquisition of a criminal record), which might be significant to first-time offenders. Nevertheless, this has been a wide-ranging and carefully detailed costing.

Because of the marked cost difference between the two reparation and mediation schemes comparisons with prosecution must not be oversimplified. For prosecution, the dangers of reductionism in reporting costs are even more acute, for there are many variable factors. This complicates the comparison with the cost of reparation and mediation.

For example, the cost of reparation and mediation in Edinburgh (£404) was considerably more than what was effectively the statistical expectation ('the best guess average') for the cost of prosecution (£195). However, prosecution would cost rather more if the accused pled not guilty at the pleading diet. For example, even if the plea was subsequently changed to guilty and legal aid was claimed, the cost of prosecution is likely to be £756. In contrast, the average cost of the comparison group (£250) was similar to the cost of reparation and mediation in Glasgow (£298).

Generally it is clear that reparation and mediation was a more costly option for simple cases. The types of case for which it cost less than prosecution were those, such as neighbourhood disputes, where the accused (and perhaps also the victim) had a desire to put their side of the story, and wanted the case to go to prosecution in order to give the dispute a public airing.

Were reparation and mediation to continue to perform the same tasks as during the study period, taking the same range of cases, and working at the same scale, it could be expected to find its aggregate costs reducing slightly as it, and the fiscals, and others with which it works, moved up their learning curves.

Developing and extending reparation and mediation

Reparation and mediation could develop and extend its remit in a number of ways, each with cost implications. An obvious development mentioned already would be for the Edinburgh scheme to increase the number of cases to approach its full capacity, and/or for other schemes to be set up which take advantage of the management and training overheads already in place.

In the next chapter there is discussion of the possible opportunities for the two schemes to receive cases directly from the police. Such an extension would reduce the costs of reparation and mediation by removing the cost to fiscals of preparing a case for prosecution. The extent of the saving can be gauged by contrasting the average cost of legal aid (£281) and the cost of prosecution (£37) for a case that pleads guilty at the pleading diet. However, in extending the referral base for the schemes, the time limitations on gathering evidence and reporting must be noted, for unless this work had been completed it would not be possible to prosecute the case at a later date should an agreement fail.

The estimated costs of prosecution apply to the least serious cases taken through the courts, those heard at district courts. Substituting reparation and mediation for prosecution of cases heard at sheriff courts would reduce criminal justice system costs, for these cases can cost considerably more to prosecute than district court cases. They take more time: for example, the average case heard in the sheriff court takes the fiscal service 86 per cent more legal and 19 per cent more administrative time. The costs of legal aid are also higher: on average, legal aid payments associated with a summary trial are 25 per cent higher in the sheriff court than in the district court. The costs of court appearances are also higher: summary trials last longer (75 minutes on average) and cost more, £3 per minute using the same basis as that used for estimating the cost of district court time (based on figures provided by the Crown Office and Scottish Courts Administration).

Allowing for the higher costs of administration, court time and legal aid, but making no adjustments to police commitments or witness payments, a sheriff summary court case that pled guilty would cost a third more ((£99 than a district court case, a case that pled guilty at the trial diet 17 per cent more (£672) and a trial case 67 per cent more (£1,542). The use of reparation and mediation with more serious cases would also have implications for downstream costs, for offenders will have been diverted from more costly disposals. For example, with the cost of prison custody averaging £56 per inmate day (excluding capital), reparation and mediation would be considerably less costly than even a custodial sentence (with associated court costs) of a week's duration. Reparation and mediation costs would probably be higher when working with more serious offences, though the increase would be modest when set alongside these sheriff court and custody costs.

Finally, a welcome development for SACRO would be to reduce the funding uncertainty for reparation and mediation, which has been more than a distraction. This would bring down the average overhead cost in the short term, and encourage the expansion and consolidation of the services in the long term. Reparation and mediation funding has an untidy history, with a sizeable proportion of income coming in the form of donations from various voluntary bodies. The savings to local authorities from a reparation and mediation service are minimal: the costs of court time in Glasgow are more than offset by revenue from fines, and local authorities do not bear the principal cost of defaulting, which is imprisonment. The reduction in the workload of the fiscal service in preparing cases for prosecution would be largely offset by the increased workload resulting from marking cases for diversion which are returned and have to be re-assessed.

Where, then, are the savings? The main savings to the criminal justice system in diverting cases away from prosecution in the direction of reparation and mediation accrue to the centrally funded Scottish Office. The Scottish Office, responsible for allocating of funds to the police and for legal aid, would benefit by 77 per cent of the estimated £195 expenditure savings on an average district court case. The Crown Office would reap savings from those cases which would have gone through to trial in the absence of the scheme.

The two SACRO reparation and mediation schemes were not *cheap* alternatives to prosecution. They supplemented the prosecution process which currently cost less than the activities and processes they replaced in a variety of circumstances, and there is scope for further efficiency and other gains in the future.

9 Conclusions

What can be learnt from the SACRO Project about the benefits of reparation and mediation as an approach within and around the criminal justice system?

Fulfilling the aims of the project

Promoting reparation as a proper objective of the criminal justice system

Most participants, victims, accused, fiscals and mediators, clearly considered reparation by the accused to be a proper objective of criminal justice in minor cases. This finding is in line with public opinion surveys which have shown significant support for reparation (for example, Wright, 1989).

Piloting reparation as an alternative to prosecution

Cases which would otherwise have been prosecuted were dealt with successfully by the project. The vast majority would have been prosecuted in the district courts. The Edinburgh scheme was designed to accept cases due to be prosecuted in the Sheriff Court and, in the early days, did so. However, such referrals were rare during the study period. There is the potential to deal with more serious cases successfully and, as discussed in Chapter Eight, there would be cost benefits of so doing.

Evidence from the comparison group and interviews suggests that a number of cases would have been unlikely to be prosecuted. The project was originally established to explore the potential role of reparation and mediation as a diversion from prosecution. Whilst broader applications of reparation and mediation were valuable, there are serious drawbacks of operating beyond diversion under current arrangements. These are discussed below.

Testing the applicability of mediation as a technique for dispute resolution within the criminal justice system

Involving a trained mediator in the resolution of a dispute between parties who knew each other helped the majority of victims and accused come to an agreement which they were able to sustain, at least for several months and without resorting to further offending. Where the parties were strangers both seemed happy to conclude the incident when the agreement had been fulfilled. Both outcomes could be regarded as successful resolutions of the dispute. Some might regard resolution as involving the reconciliation of the parties or the resolution of the emotional and psychological impact of the offence on victim and accused. The project appears to have been less successful in helping parties relieve themselves of the emotional burdens of the offence, particularly when victim and accused were in regular and close contact. Often, tensions, dislike and even feuds continued after the involvement of the mediator, even if there had been no further offending. This is not unique to the SACRO scheme, but reflects the fact that considerable intervention might be required to tackle the underlying problems between such parties.

For the victim and accused to reach a full resolution of the incident and aftermath would probably require greater mediator involvement. In some of the neighbour disputes a considerable amount of time and work would probably be involved. This would be unrealistic within the existing resources and remit of the project. However, on the occasions where mediators had become involved in complex disputes, project staff and fiscals regarded the input as very successful. Not all cases, however, required a large amount of mediation. In a small number of cases, mediators simply informed the fiscal that the parties had already resolved their differences. Thus the project was able to support people's own attempts at dispute resolution.

Providing a service to victims

Through reparation and mediation victims were offered a service which they clearly appreciated and valued, including being consulted about how the case should be resolved and receiving the compensation requested. Many found contact with the mediator to be helpful and saw reparation as a fair and just response to the offence. If victims wished no further action or regarded the case as serious enough to warrant prosecution this information was conveyed to the fiscal who usually took action which reflected the victim's views.

Providing a constructive and challenging response to the accused

Procedures were adopted by which the fiscal oversaw agreements to ensure that they were fair to both parties and broadly comparable with likely court sanctions. Accused were generally required to make amends which were qualitatively and quantitatively compatible with the damage or loss suffered by the victim, including inconvenience or distress where victims felt this was important.

In some instances accused agreed to pay considerable sums to the victim and those on low incomes could find repayments very taxing, even when paying in instalments. The payments could serve as a regular reminder of the consequences of the offence. There were, of course, accused who found little problem in making compensation. Mediators and fiscals tried to ensure that agreements were not only fair to both parties, but also were realistic in terms of the accused's financial situation. Agreements involving behavioural undertakings could be equally demanding, with accused required to 'behave' for periods of up to six months. Offences which were related to ongoing disputes, say between neighbours, could be particularly demanding.

Whilst most agreements were largely comparable with likely court sanctions, referral to the project meant that the accused concerned avoided what was often regarded as a humiliating and shameful court appearance. It was this experience rather than a resulting sentence which most accused were anxious to avoid. As well as public humiliation many feared that a subsequent conviction could lead to loss of a job or job opportunities and that this would have an adverse effect on their lives. It should be noted that a large number of accused had no previous experience of the criminal justice system. Unfortunately there were insufficient face-to-face meetings to draw any conclusions about the potential for direct mediation. However, the SACRO project achieved a high level of acceptance and successful completion rates using mainly indirect mediation. Research on other schemes (Marshall and Merry, 1990) shows that well-planned and conducted meetings between victims and accused can be very beneficial to both parties.

Reducing the pressure on the courts

The project obviously removed from the courts cases which would otherwise have been prosecuted. However, even if all referrals had been diversions, the numbers involved would have been too small to make a noticeable impact on the workloads of the relevant courts. On the other hand, it makes sense to consider reparation and mediation as another piece in the jigsaw of alternatives to prosecution. As such the project filled a major gap. Unlike all other alternatives reparation and mediation allowed the fiscal to divert cases where the public interest lay largely in compensating the victim. Some cases were dealt with which would otherwise not have been prosecuted. This represents an expansion of the involvement of the criminal justice system. There are associated cost implications of this, possible problems for the accused and an increase in the workload of the criminal justice system. It could also be argued that whilst generally regarded as a problem, 'net widening' can have a positive impact in this instance (Warner, 1992). Here it offers a response to offences otherwise judged not serious enough to necessitate prosecution by the fiscals but where victims feel some action is necessary. Individual victims' perceptions and experiences of the impact of crime can be drawn into the public interest equation.

If 'pressure' is defined more widely, it could be argued (and indeed was by some fiscals and project staff) that the project reduces pressure on the courts by removing cases particularly unsuited to an adversarial approach, those related to neighbour and family disputes. Such cases are often difficult to accommodate within formal criminal proceedings and were regarded by some as civil disputes which had resulted in an offence. The public interest lay in reducing tensions rather than in punishing the accused. Fiscals, mediators and victims and accused were of the opinion that such cases were usually better dealt with without recourse to formal proceedings.

The costs of reparation and mediation

The study by Knapp and Netten, described in Chapter Eight, suggests that the reparation and mediation project did not involve savings for the criminal justice system, particularly in Edinburgh. The lower cost of successful referral compared with prosecution found in Glasgow arose mainly because the latter was operating at full capacity. In Glasgow Knapp and Netten found that successful referral to the scheme was broadly comparable, in financial terms, to prosecution if the accused plead guilty at the pleading diet. Where a not guilty plea would otherwise have been entered, for example where the accused wanted both sides of a story to be aired in court, referral to reparation and mediation could be considerably cheaper than prosecution. Where the accused simply made reparation to the victim, prosecution was cheaper than referral.

Chapter Eight considered in detail the costs of the projects and suggestions are made as to how the costs of referral could be reduced within the existing arrangements. The study by Knapp and Netten suggests that the cost of referral in Edinburgh would be reduced if the scheme had sufficient referrals to operate at full capacity. Also, if more serious cases were to be referred, including those marked for prosecution in the sheriff court, there could be cost savings to the criminal justice system. It is understood that the Edinburgh scheme has been referred such cases, unfortunately outwith the monitoring period, and that these have been successfully resolved. The number of referrals in Edinburgh has also increased. The scheme in Glasgow is no longer operational. Thus there is potential to reduce the costs of diversion to reparation and mediation and the potential to develop this approach further.

The potential of reparation and mediation

A growing body of research and experience from Europe and the United States suggests that there are considerable potential benefits to be had from involving victim and accused in reparation and mediation (for example Marshall and Merry, 1990; Dixon, undated; KARB, 1989, 1990; Ruddick, 1989; Young, 1986). 'Reparation and mediation' can be used to describe a wide range of approaches and arrangements, including programmes based largely on offenders paying compensation through a scheme rather than the courts; those which offer considerable counselling, with almost therapeutic intervention; and those set up specifically to reduce the use of custody.

It is nevertheless difficult to draw firm conclusions on the basis of research and writings on reparation and mediation. First, there has been a lack of conceptual clarity in the terms used to describe schemes and their function. The term reparation and mediation has been used to describe schemes with varied aims, methods and principles. Secondly it is not always the case that the projects necessarily implement the programme as planned (see McIvor, 1990b). Thirdly, the impact and shape of the general reparation and mediation approach are heavily influenced by schemes' location and by situational factors. Not all studies have separated out the general approach to dispute resolution from the function and location of schemes.

With these points in mind this section explores two issues. First, the potential benefits and drawbacks of the general approach are discussed. Secondly, the implications of siting reparation and mediation as a diversion from formal criminal justice and the potential for wider application are examined.

Potential benefits for the parties

As discussed in the introduction, direct mediation, where victim and offender meet face-to-face in the presence of a trained mediator, offers the best chance of resolving the offence for all parties. Whilst we know little about the specific processes and interactions which enhance the effectiveness of a mediation meeting, when direct mediation works it offers both parties a chance to air their experiences and grievances, to ask questions of the other and have these answered and to move beyond the offence (Marshall, 1992; Umbreit, 1992; Chupp, 1989). Reparation by the offender, whilst material, becomes symbolic of the offender's willingness to make amends to the victim and of the victim's forgiveness. Satisfaction for victims and accused appears to relate more to the quality of the process and interactions, not to outcomes alone, placing the emphasis on the development of and insistence on good practice (Tyler, 1988).

Not all victims necessarily wish to meet the accused. Straight reparation, without direct mediation, has been little researched but is generally cited as less effective and satisfactory than face-to-face contact. The present study suggests that for many victims of minor crime, having the opportunity to receive compensation for loss or damage, which might include an apology and explanation, is adequate but may not completely resolve underlying tensions.

Where the parties are in dispute and living in close proximity with regular contact, the offence can be regarded as a symptom of the underlying problems which mediation can help the parties face and resolve. The project demonstrated that mediation can be effective in such complex cases. Despite the small numbers the evaluation suggested that cases involving family members and ex-partners were particularly difficult to resolve. Given the intensity and high emotional tone of such disputes this is not surprising. Whilst such cases were frequently resolved to the satisfaction of criminal justice staff (that is no prosecution and agreements fulfilled), from the point of view of the parties, difficulties often continued. At the same time, none of the respondents involved in such cases would have wished the case to have gone to court.

The benefits of the SACRO project lay for the accused largely in the diversionary aspects. In this study a number of accused welcomed the opportunity to make good the damage and some wanted to reassure the victims (and probably themselves) that, despite their actions, they were not criminals. Whether or not these accused would have regarded reparation and mediation so positively were they not offered the incentive of avoiding a court appearance is a moot point. Chupp (1989) suggests that voluntary mediation and reparation offers both parties a positive experience. The accused involved in the SACRO project were mainly first offenders with little previous direct experience of the criminal justice system and their responses appear different from those surveyed in other research who often had lengthy criminal records. The project offered accused an opportunity to close the incident and hopefully allowed them to return to a 'law-abiding' self image.

Potential benefits to the criminal justice system

One important benefit of the SACRO project was that it was regarded by all groups involved as a sensible, fair and just approach to minor crime. The level of consensus was striking. Where the offence related to a dispute, fiscals, victims and accused regarded mediation as a better solution than court proceedings which could exacerbate the situation. Parallels were drawn with the increasing use of a conciliation-based approach in the civil courts, particularly where access to and custody of children are involved. Where the victim had sustained loss or damage, reparation made directly by the accused was seen as a fair and effective response. Reparation and mediation was widely regarded as a better solution to minor crime than court proceedings which were heavy-handed and expensive responses. Victims and accused saw formal prosecution as a means of drawing problematic behaviour to the attention of the authorities both to protect themselves and the community and to ensure the accused was punished or treated as required.

Having a credible and respected justice system is important in its own right. All groups clearly saw prosecution as important but in a more limited range of cases than is currently the case. At the same time, taking no further action could also be regarded as damaging the credibility of the criminal justice system and the agencies involved.

There are also the practical benefits of enhancing the credibility of the justice system in general and involving more victims in the consideration of justice. The increasing criminal justice emphasis on serious offences and offenders has meant that minor crime is less likely to be responded to, at least from the victim's perspective. The victim will hear little about the progress and action taken by agencies unless required as a witness, although some police forces do keep victims informed of progress. If the victims of crime see no action taken they are less likely to report offences in future and less willing to participate in the criminal justice system at various points (Volpe, 1989). The SACRO project not only ensured that the victims concerned were made aware that notice had been taken of their case but offered victims the opportunity to influence the response and to receive compensation of some kind. Criminal justice agencies rely on victims to be aware of and deal with crime. As Knapp and Netten's study suggests, there is also the possibility that diversion to reparation and mediation could involve financial savings for the criminal justice system.

The drawbacks of reparation and mediation

Few would argue against the victims of crime receiving a better deal from criminal justice, regardless of how criminal justice officials consider the severity of the offence. Criticisms outlined in the introduction to this report include the allegation that reparation and mediation schemes do not really pay attention to the victim but focus primarily on saving criminal justice costs; provide mitigation for offenders; bolster an ailing justice system; and endanger the rights of vulnerable groups by removing their problems from formal court proceedings to the informal and essentially hidden arena of diversion. Finally, schemes have been criticised for extending the scope of social control to those who would not have been the focus of formal intervention. All these points relate to the way reparation and mediation schemes have been developed and apply to formal and informal diversion schemes of various kinds.

Such problems are not necessarily inherent in the general approach. This is not to deny there are problems to be overcome in the area of victim-offender mediation. Projects have problems in identifying what mediation styles and approaches lead to desirable and undesirable outcomes. Research is currently being conducted in this area which will hopefully provide guidance (Umbreit, 1992; Messmer, 1992; Chupp, 1989). There are difficulties in balancing working with victims to help them consider direct mediation, with pressurising them to participate. There are also problems in trying to prevent offenders from continuing to neutralise and minimise the impact of their actions on the victim and from attempting to blame victims (Messmer, 1992; Davis, 1992). An approach which seeks to shed light on good practice should help alleviate these problems.

On a practical level, if victims do report more offences and if more victims are to be offered reparation and mediation, there will be financial and workload costs involved in this extension of justice. There is a balance to be struck between having a more credible and fairer justice system and the costs that could be involved. It would also be crucial to ensure that the rights and interests of accused persons were not eroded by any developments. These points are discussed in more detail below.

Some writers have pointed to the lack of impact that reparation and mediation projects have had on traditional justice systems. Davis (1992) has said schemes remain marginal and so have not challenged what are basically retributive justice systems. It would be unreasonable to expect a small, pilot project to change the face of criminal justice overnight but the SACRO project illustrated that reparation and mediation can work successfully in a Scottish context and has the potential for wider application.

The SACRO project was developed primarily as a means of diverting relatively minor crimes from prosecution. This influenced the location and procedures of the project. Whilst run by a voluntary agency, the project took referrals almost exclusively from the procurator fiscal. The fiscal retained the right throughout to prosecute the case if either party refused or was not satisfied with the progress or (theoretically) the outcome of the case. Fiscals selected cases where the public interest allowed diversion and where this was judged likely to be desirable from various points of view.

Operating as a diversion scheme, fiscal oversight and control was essential in order to balance different needs and interests, but the diversionary focus of the project influenced all aspects of reparation and mediation (Warner, 1992). It must be stressed that many of the problems raised below are found in other diversion schemes (see for example Stedward and Millar,1989; Cooke, 1989) and are not inherent in reparation and mediation per se. Rather they relate to the difficulty of ensuring that diversions from formal proceedings only operate as such and on ensuring that the safeguards and protection of interests afforded by formal proceedings are at least not eroded when cases are dealt with informally.

The boundaries of diversion

Diversions and alternatives of various kinds have regularly been found to extend their operations beyond those cases which would have previously been dealt with by the formal system. This 'net widening' has the effect of exposing more accused to sanctions and interventions and so of widening and strengthening the net of social control.

As discussed in the introduction the range of alternatives to prosecution has expanded over recent years. Fiscals no longer simply mark for prosecution or non-prosecution but have available a repertoire of responses along a continuum between formal proceedings and taking no further action whatsoever. This makes it increasingly difficult to categorise cases using the simple prosecution/non-prosecution dichotomy, regardless of the particular diversion under investigation. Reparation and mediation has also had the effect of drawing the victims of minor crime into considerations regarding prosecution. Whilst the impact of an offence on the victim was originally a factor in the fiscals' considerations of the public interest, the development of the SACRO project has provided fiscals not only with a means of recognising the impact on the victim without formal proceedings, but also with greater feedback on the needs and views of the victims of minor crime. Fiscals also received more information on the complexities and histories of a case outwith a court setting. Solutions could then be better tailored to the specific instances involved and the process of responding to minor crime become more 'humanised'

These two factors are likely to increase the tendency towards net-widening already present in diversion schemes. It is therefore important to consider the way that the impact of reparation and mediation has been influenced by its role as a diversion from prosecution in Scotland.

In order to protect the rights and interests of the accused and the proper functioning of the criminal justice system procedures have been adopted to attempt to restrict the intervention of the criminal justice system. Fiscals increasingly regard prosecution as a last resort and as too severe a response to much minor crime. Alternatives offer responses to an offence without recourse to court and both bridge and create the gulf between a straight non-prosecution (no further action) and prosecution. Alternatives can be offered unconditionally to accused persons, where a refusal or failure to comply does not lead to further action (waived prosecution), or conditionally, with a prosecution following if the fiscal is not satisfied with the accused's response. Diversions such as the SACRO project which operate under deferred prosecution are better described as replacing formal sanctions if the case was successfully completed. Where a case was unsuccessfully referred, then the fiscal would generally prosecute the case in the usual way. This expansion appears to allow a more sensitive individualised response, whilst at the same time the fiscal's role was such that he or she could ensure a degree of consistency across cases.

There is tension between the need to restrict access to reparation and mediation only to cases which would otherwise have been prosecuted and extending the justice system to cases where mediation between the parties or reparation to the victim is judged the best way of responding to the offence. By operating reparation and mediation only as a diversion from prosecution it is not possible to reconcile these different interests. Inevitably, some accused will be drawn into the criminal justice system net in order to benefit victims; and to protect the accused, other victims will not be offered reparation and mediation.

Two further factors have to be balanced. First, there is the need to control the sanctions imposed on the accused should the referral fail; and second, the victim's needs for action to be taken and to receive compensation. Again, the two could be reconciled by making a clear separation between the use of reparation and mediation as a diversion and other uses; for example, as an open-access service to the victims of crime.

The limits of diversion

The focus on diversion in the SACRO scheme and others has had the effect of placing severe limitations on the use of reparation and mediation as an approach within the criminal justice system. The following section explores the impact on victims, accused and the criminal justice system of operating reparation and mediation as a diversion.

Victims and access to reparation and mediation. Reparation and mediation projects have been found acceptable and beneficial to many groups of victims. Umbreit in the United States reports that the victims of very serious offences have found direct mediation a valuable and therapeutic experience (Umbreit, 1989; Gustafson, 1990). At the other extreme some victims involved in what may be described as 'trivial ' offences may nevertheless suffer a great deal and may find a meeting with the offender beneficial. Because of other aspects of the public interest only a relatively narrow band of cases could be diverted from prosecution. The factors which allow diversion are generally not connected with the impact on the victim but with the offence and the offender. Police reports generally contain little information on the victim, reflecting the general focus of the criminal justice system. This means that reparation and mediation is only available to limited numbers of victims (and then only if other factors allow) and access is not initially on the basis of victim need.

Research on the experiences of victims shows clearly that people's responses to an offence and their recovery from it vary considerably and that the preparedness for and usefulness of meeting with an accused also varies (Lurigio and Resick, 1990; Shapland et al, 1985). By restricting access to diversion from prosecution victims are offered reparation and mediation at a particular point in the criminal justice timetable, not necessarily when they would be most open to mediation or when they could most benefit. Also, because the SACRO project was limited to two geographical areas only victims of crimes committed in these areas were likely to be considered. In the SACRO schemes there were limits and constraints on diverting cases to reparation and mediation. These restricted the extent to which reparation and mediation was offered as a service to the victims of crime. While these were the result of valid criminal justice concerns the service was limited as a consequence and therefore denied to victims who might have found involvement in the project beneficial.

Access for accused. Little is known about the extent to which offenders desire to make amends and express remorse, independent of any mitigation of sanctions which might occur as a result. In this study a few accused had offered to make amends, apologise and pay compensation before contact from the project. It is not possible to estimate how often victims or police stop pursuing further action after an accused has taken steps to make good the damage. Many people are discouraged from taking such action in case by doing so they incriminate themselves and preempt a court decision. As Zehr (1989) argues, the state has taken over the conflict between the victim and accused and the responsibility for determining the sanctions. The state punishes the accused, rather than attempting to encourage them to face the consequences of their behaviour and to make good the loss. It is possible that first offenders, offenders with an ongoing relationship to the victim, or those who have a brief or broken criminal history are more open to reparation and mediation; but there is at present, no evidence on this.

Writers such as Wright (1992) and Zehr (1989) have argued that reparation and mediation offers accused persons a clearer understanding of the impact of their actions and an opportunity to earn acceptance in the community. Regardless of what sanctions the state wishes to impose as punishment or treatment of the offender there seems to be no reason to limit the chance to close an incident and to reintegrate into the community only to those who commit occasional, minor offences. It could be argued that serious, repeat offenders are more in need of such opportunities. Within the context of diversion, however, the focus is on protecting the rights of the accused and avoiding net-widening and so access has to be limited for the reasons outlined above. It is worth noting that in Japan, an apology from the accused or her or his family is expected (Haley, 1992).

The criminal justice system. The comments of the fiscals in Chapter Six and their willingness to make referrals to reparation and mediation show that they saw reparation and mediation as a valuable approach in the justice system. It was evident that fiscals also perceived a broader role for reparation and mediation beyond diversion. This was particularly the case in their views on neighbour and family disputes where tensions finally led to an offence serious enough to warrant prosecution. Some fiscals judged that early referral of such cases could help prevent offending. In some minor fraud, dishonesty or criminal damage cases fiscals reported they were unwilling to prosecute for small amounts but would have liked the victim to be compensated. However, because a prosecution was likely for refusal or breach, fiscals were obviously reluctant to refer borderline cases.

Reparation and mediation: beyond diversion

There is a body of opinion which criticises the retributive nature of traditional justice for its lack of effectiveness, confused, conflicting and often implicit aims and its emphasis on punishment. Writers such as Wright (1992) and Marshall (1988) in England, Mackay (1988) in Scotland and Zehr (l985) in the United States regard traditional justice systems in the West as in a state of crisis. What is advocated is a change of paradigm (Zehr, 1989) away from a justice system based on retribution to one based on restoration of balance. In a recent paper, Wright argues (1992, p.l):

> The concept of restorative justice is simple. The scales of justice are no longer seen as balancing the harm done by the offender with further harm inflicted *on* the offender; that only adds to the total amount of harm ... Instead the harm is balanced by offering support to the victim, and requiring the offender to make amends, with help from the community if necessary.

Within such a system, reparation and mediation offers a means of balancing the needs of the victim, the accused and the community. Reparation and mediation can also be of value within what is essentially a retributive, that is a punishment-focused, and adversarial system. Being required to make amends either directly to the victim or to the community (for example, doing work or making a donation for charity or community service) requires the individual offender to face the consequences of her or his actions and compensates the victim. Some researchers have suggested that direct mediation might also reduce recidivism (Marshall, 1992) although the evidence is not clear cut.

Currently, the SACRO project only accepts cases which the fiscal judges can be diverted from prosecution. This means that very serious offences and those where prosecution is regarded as essential are excluded.

Research in the United States (Umbreit, 1989b) and England (Marshall and Merry, 1990) suggests that some victims of serious crimes can benefit greatly from direct mediation. It also seems likely that with support and advocacy for the victim greater numbers would wish to meet the offender. The potential benefits of referring victims severely traumatised by an offence to reparation and mediation are possibly greater than for those less affected. An example of such an argument can be found in Gehm's (1992) discussion of mediation, forgiveness and criminal justice. By operating reparation and mediation only as a diversion for minor crime, victims of serious crimes and those severely affected by what are deemed trivial crimes are denied the option of reparation and mediation. By separating access to reparation and mediation and criminal justice sanctions victim need could become the determinant of referral. Punishment of the accused and other functions of the criminal justice system could be unaffected by meeting the needs of victims.

Such a scheme could operate independently of the courts focusing on the needs of victims to express their views and receive explanations and understanding. Marshall and Merry (1990) suggest that offenders might be less inclined to participate without an incentive and care would have to be taken to ensure that victims are not re-victimised when an accused refuses mediation. Others have pointed out that such schemes are of necessity limited to those cases where an accused is apprehended, and that victims of crimes where no accused is caught also have needs and problems related to the offence which should be addressed. Victim support schemes obviously have an important role to play in such cases, providing a range of services and approaches geared to supporting victims in various ways. Liaison with local victim support schemes could play an important role in identifying those victims who could benefit from reparation and mediation.

Launay and Murray (1989) evaluated a scheme in which the victims of house burglary met young offenders in a local young offender institution who were serving sentences for comparable burglaries. Group meetings were face-to-face and in the presence of trained mediators. Victims were referred by the local victim support scheme and police crime prevention officer. Both victims and offenders were found to benefit from meeting as a group as long as the offences involved were similar (see also Northmere, 1988).

Where accused are identified and are willing to be referred for reparation and mediation a project similar to the SACRO scheme could deal with voluntary referrals. The Leeds reparation and mediation scheme reports cases where mediation has taken place between sentenced offenders and victims (Leeds Reparation Project, 1987). Referrals could come from victim support, offenders or prisons on a voluntary basis. Such an extension would involve extra costs but it would represent a serious attempt to develop victim services rather than an attempt to reduce pressures and costs of the formal justice system.

Extending reparation and mediation as a diversion from formal proceedings

There is scope for the Edinburgh scheme to divert more serious offences than at present, particularly referrals of cases facing prosecution in the Sheriff Court. Not only would this allow reparation and mediation to be made more widely available to victims but, as Knapp and Netten discuss in Chapter Eight, there would be greater cost savings were Edinburgh to receive such referrals.

The Glasgow court system is organised differently. In Glasgow, there are four stipendiary magistrates who sit in the district courts and have powers similar to sheriffs. This means that the district court in Glasgow deals with summary prosecutions which would be handled in the Sheriff Court in Edinburgh. Even though the Glasgow project operated at full capacity fiscals estimated that referrals could potentially treble.

Reparation and mediation schemes have also been used to divert offenders from custody or to reduce the severity of custodial sentences, and their close proximity to the formal criminal justice system has been said to lead towards a bias towards the offender (Davis, 1992; Young, 1989). The impact of schemes which operate following conviction but prior to sentence appears small. Many of these have aimed at reducing the levels of custody. Where such schemes were in operation, Marshall and Merry (1990) found a shift away from fines towards compensation orders, probation and community service in about 18 per cent of cases referred to projects in magistrates courts, and 25 per cent of cases in crown courts. There was little impact on the use of custody. Whilst there might be some financial savings in such circumstances there are also important questions about the benefits to victims.

Reparation and mediation and minor crime

Victims in cases judged not serious enough to warrant further action can nonetheless be severely affected by the offence and could benefit from reparation and mediation. Trivial offences have to be excluded from referral to the SACRO project at present because of its role as a diversion. Loosening the links between reparation and mediation and formal actions and sanctions would allow the wider availability of reparation and mediation.

Waived prosecution. Under waived prosecution, the fiscal foregoes the right to prosecute the case when it is referred outwith the service. This means that should an accused refuse or fail to comply with the fiscal's proposal, no action can be taken. If reparation and mediation were to be offered in this way then appropriate cases could be referred even if the fiscal would not otherwise have prosecuted the case. Under voluntary conditions, it might be expected that accused would be less likely to cooperate with reparation and mediation and victims could be disadvantaged and re-victimised. Steps would have to be taken to support such victims as discussed earlier.

Police referral. Many of the juvenile-based schemes in England and Wales are operated by the police in conjunction with cautioning schemes. The police-based schemes have tended to be found problematic in that they offer little mediation or service to victims and focus more on making an impact on offending. There is also one similar scheme operating with adults. If the offender makes reparation a caution is given and the police do not send a report of the offence to the Crown Prosecution Service. In the current study there was anecdotal evidence from victims and accused that police sometimes operated a form of reparation and mediation on an occasional and informal basis. In some instances police had been called out to disturbances involving neighbours or family members on a number of occasions before an offence necessitating a report to the fiscal occurred. Interviewees reported calling the police for various reasons, including fear and anger, and as some accused maintained, spite and revenge. The police are frequently regarded and used as sources of authority in the community, called in during a dispute (including those between strangers). Obviously submitting a report to the fiscal will not necessarily be appropriate in all cases. The potential for the use of mediation skills and resources by community-based police is clear.

Project staff in Glasgow and Edinburgh have been approached by local police interested both in acquiring mediation skills and in offering reparation and mediation as a response to minor incidents. In cases where offences or sums involved are very minor, and where a report to the fiscal is not essential, reparation and mediation could be a useful response as long as extreme care is taken to control the actions taken if the referral is unsuccessful.

As discussed above, care would be required to ensure that accused persons would not face greater sanctions should they refuse or fail to comply with a referral. Police could either make an informal referral, with no sanctions applied for non-compliance or make a formal referral with the condition that a report be sent to the fiscal if the offer of reparation and mediation is refused. Informal referral could be useful in the early stages of a dispute to prevent escalation, leading to formal referral if this proved unsuccessful. A clear separation between the functions of reparation and mediation as a method of crime prevention and as an early form of diversion is essential to safeguard the accused and the credibility of the criminal justice system.

Beyond criminal justice: community mediation

There are across Europe and the United States reparation and mediation projects based in the community. These offer dispute resolution and mediation to various agencies and individuals. Some operate purely as a community resource, taking largely self-referrals. There appears to be a tendency for schemes which accept criminal justice referrals to have a bias towards agency rather than voluntary referrals (see for example, Iivari, 1992; Gronfors, 1992). Community mediation schemes in England have not been thoroughly researched and take time to become established as a community resource. It is difficult to assess the likely demand for such services from individuals. Project staff in Edinburgh did have at least one instance of a self-referral from an ex-client when new problems arose with a neighbour. Some resource of this kind might be of value. FIRM (1989a and b) reports the continuing development of mediation as a means of dispute resolution in a wide variety of contexts. Projects have been established in England in schools, communities and workplaces and have dealt successfully with a range of disputes and conflicts. This could lead to greater demand and use of mediation resources.

Organising reparation and mediation

Independent reparation and mediation projects may be better able to balance the interests of victims and accused. The closer the project to the criminal justice system the greater the pressures to conform to the needs and demands of the system, potentially at the expense of the victims. (Marshall and Merry, 1990; Davis, 1992). The SACRO project was sufficiently independent to allow a balanced approach to victim and accused, but only dealt with a very narrow band of cases, offering reparation and mediation at a point convenient to the criminal justice system. A problem of increasing the distance between a project and the criminal justice system is that this can marginalise reparation and mediation, reducing its relevance to and impact on formal criminal justice, with consequent difficulties in obtaining sufficient numbers of referrals.

It is important to ensure that clear distinctions are drawn between the different functions undertaken by reparation and mediation. As outlined earlier, reparation and mediation is an approach to crime which can be operated at different points.

The SACRO project clearly offered a service to victims which the majority found acceptable and valuable. However, several advocates of victims' rights (for example, Reeves, 1989), have suggested that to provide a full and fair service to victims referral to reparation and mediation should be on the basis of victims' needs and wishes. Such a service should also be made at the point the victim feels appropriate rather than when convenient for the criminal justice system. The SACRO project was established originally to explore the potential of reparation and mediation as a diversion from prosecution. This has meant that cases were only referred when judged suitable by the fiscal and then only at the point at which prosecution was being considered. Thus the service to victims provided by the SACRO schemes was necessarily limited and the criteria for referral based primarily on criminal justice concerns.

These different strands have to be balanced. Some fiscals felt that they would consider referring a case which would not definitely have been prosecuted. Whilst this offered advantages for the victim there were clear dangers to the accused who, should he or she refuse to participate or breach an agreement, could face prosecution.

In conclusion

There was a clear consensus in this study that reparation and mediation is a valuable and fair approach to minor and possibly more serious crime. The costs can be broadly favourable when compared to prosecution and the benefits considerable. The schemes did not fully explore the potential of direct mediation between victims and accused which could lead to a fuller resolution of the impact of crime.

Since the completion of the evaluation, the Glasgow scheme has closed because of lack of funds. The Edinburgh scheme continues to operate and the project manager has reported considerable interest in the development of new services, including those for the police and in other locations. This study has shown that the two schemes operated successfully in two very different locations and with different mediators to aid the development of reparation and mediation. It is to be hoped that these resources can be used further in expanding schemes which this study has shown can benefit all who participate in them.

References

Barr, H (1971) *Volunteers in Prison Aftercare,* National Institute for Social Work, no 20 London.

Brown, M and Murphy, G (1987) The Victim and Direct Reparation, *Probation Journal*, vol 34, no 3, pp 101-102.

Christie, N (1977) Conflicts as Property, *British Journal of Criminology*, vol 17, pp 1-15.

Chupp, M (1989) Reconciliation Procedures and Rationales, in Wright, M and Galaway, B (eds) *Mediation and Criminal Justice*, Sage, London.

Connor, A (1989) *Volunteering and Unemployment: A Literature Review*, Scottish Office, Central Research Unit Paper, Edinburgh.

Cooke, D (1989) *Treatment as an Alternative to Prosecution Volume 1 - Diversion to the Douglas Inch Clinic*, Scottish Office, Central Research Unit, Edinburgh.

Crown Office (no date given) *Prosecution of Crime in Scotland,* HMSO, Edinburgh.

Crown Prosecution Service *Annual Report 1988/89,* HMSO, London.

Davis, G (1989) Report of an Observation Study, *Repairing the Damage: The First National Symposium on Mediation and Criminal Justice*, Forum for Initiatives in Reparation and Mediation,[1] Beaconsfield.

(1) FIRM is now 'Mediation UK., Bristol.

Davis, G (1992) Reparation in the UK: Dominant Themes and Neglected Themes, in Messmer, H and Otto, H-U (eds) *Restorative Justice on Trial,* Kluwer Academic Publishers, Dordrecht.

Dixon, P (unpubl.) *The South Yorkshire Mediation Scheme,* South Yorkshire Probation Service, Sheffield.

Ewing, G (1990) Personal communication, 6 June.

FIRM (1989a) *Directory of Mediation Projects and Conflict Resolution Services 1989,* Forum for Initiatives in Reparation and Mediation, Beaconsfield.

FIRM (1989b) *The Need for Community Mediation Services,* Forum for Intiatives in Reparation and Mediation, Occasional Paper, no 5, Beaconsfield.

Galaway, B (1992) The New Zealand Experience Implementing the Reparation Sentence, in Messmer, H and Otto, H-U (eds) *Restorative Justice on Trial,* Kluwer Academic Publishers, Dordrecht.

Gehm, J (1992) The Function of Forgiveness in the Criminal Justice System, in Messmer, H and Otto, H-U (eds) *Restorative Justice on Trial,* Kluwer Academic Publishers, Dordrecht.

Gronfors, M (1992) Mediation - A Romantic Ideal or a Workable Alternative?, in Messmer, H and Otto, H-U (eds) *Restorative Justice on Trial,* Kluwer Academic Publishers, Dordrecht.

Gustafson, D (1990) Debunking the Myths: Victim Offender Reconciliation in Serious Crime, *Victim-Offender Mediation,* vol 2, no 1, pp 8-9.

Haley, J (1989) Confession, Repentance and Absolution, in Wright, M and Galaway, B (eds) *Mediation and Criminal Justice,* Sage, London.

Haley, J (1992) Victim-Offender Mediation: Japanese and American Comparisons, in Messmer, H and Otto, H-U (eds) *Restorative Justice on Trial,* Kluwer Academic Publishers, Dordrecht.

Hartmann, A (1992) Victim-Offender Reconciliation-Program and Outcomes, in Messmer, H and Otto, H-U (eds) *Restorative Justice on Trial,* Kluwer Academic Publishers, Dordrecht.

Hillenbrand, S (1990) Restitution and Victim Rights in the 1990s, in Lurigio, A, Skogan, A and Davis, R (eds) *Victims of Crime: Problems, Policies and Programs,* Sage, New York.

HMSO (1980) *The Motorist and Fixed Penalties - First Report of the Stewart Committee,* Cmnd 8027, HMSO, Edinburgh.

HMSO (1983) *Keeping Offenders out of Court: Further Alternatives to Prosecution - Second Report of the Stewart Committee,* Cmnd 8958, HMSO, Edinburgh.

HMSO (1989) *Punishment, Custody and the Community,* Cmnd 424, HMSO, London.

HMSO (1990) *The Victims' Charter: A Statement of the Rights of Victims of Crime,* HMSO, London.
HMSO (1990) *Crime, Justice and Protecting the Public*, Cmnd 965, HMSO, London.
HM Treasury (1990) *Report of the CISD Involvement in the Work Measurement of the PF Service,* Internal Report, Work Measurement and Productivity Unit of the Consultancy and Inspection Service Division, HM Treasury.
Iivari, J (1992) The Process of Mediation: A Special Reference to the Question 'How to Get Cases for Mediation', in Messmer, H and Otto, H-U (eds) *Restorative Justice on Trial*, Kluwer Academic Publishers, Dordrecht.
KARB (Kettering Adult Reparation Bureau) (1989) *First Annual Report,* Northamptonshire Probation Service, Northampton.
KARB (1990) *Report of the Second Year,* Northamptonshire Probation Service, Northampton.
Knapp, M R J (1990a) Cost, *Administration in Social Work*, vol 15, pp 1-2.
Knapp, M R J, McCrone, P, Drury, C and Gould, E (1992) Intermediate Treatment: Using Client Characteristics to Predict Costs, in Netten, A and Beecham, J (eds) *Costing Community Care: Theory and Practice,* Ashgate, Aldershot.
Knapp, M R J and Fenyo, A (1988) Prison Costs: Why the Variation?, *Home Office Research Bulletin,* vol 25, pp 9-13.
Knapp, M R J, McIvor, G and Robertson, E (1992) The Comparative Costs of Community Service and Custody in Scotland, *Howard Journal of Criminal Justice,* vol 31, no 1, pp 8-30.
Launay, G and Murray, P (1989) Victim/Offender Groups, in Wright, M and Galaway, B (eds) *Mediation and Criminal Justice*, Sage, London.
Lawrence, P (1990) *Personal Communication*, June 1990.
Leeds Reparation Project (1987) *Report on Experimental Period 1 May 1985 - 30 April 1987,* West Yorkshire Probation Service, Leeds.
Lurigio, A J and Resick, P (1990) Healing the Psychological Wounds of Criminal Victimization: Predicting Postcrime Distress and Recovery, in Lurigio, A et al (eds) *Victims of Crime: Problems, Policies and Programmes*, Sage, New York.
MacFarlane, J (1990) Personal communication, 9th October.
McIvor, G (1990a) *Community Service Orders: Assessing the Benefit to the Community,* Social Work Research Centre, University of Stirling.
McIvor, G (1990b) *Sanctions for Serious or Persistent Offenders: A Review of the Literature,* Social Work Research Centre, University of Stirling.
Mackay, R (1986) *The Place of Mediation and Reparation in the Criminal Justice System,* MSc Dissertation, Edinburgh University.

Mackay, R (1988) *Reparation in Criminal Justice*, SACRO, Edinburgh.

Mackay, R (1989) The Resuscitation of Assythment: Restoring Reparation to the Scottish Justice System, Paper given at the Socio-Legal Conference, Edinburgh, 11th April 1989.

Maguire, M and Corbett, C (1987) *The Effects of Crime and the Work of Victim Support Schemes*, Gower, Aldershot.

Maguire, M and Shapland, J (1990) The 'Victims Movement' in Europe, in Lurigio, A et al (eds), *Victims of Crime: Problems, Policies and Programs,* Sage, New York.

Marshall, T (1988) The Use of Conflict Resolution in the Criminal Justice System including Pre-Trial, Paper given at SACRO Conference on Conflict Resolution, October 1988, Edinburgh.

Marshall, T (1989) Towards a New Justice System: Repairing the Damage, *First National Symposium on Mediation in Criminal Justice,* Forum for Initiatives in Mediation, Beaconsfield.

Marshall, T (1992) Restorative Justice on Trial in Britain, in Messmer, H and Otto, H-U (eds) *Restorative Justice on Trial*, Kluwer Academic Publishers, Dordrecht.

Marshall, T and Merry, S (1990) *Crime and Accountability: Victim/Offender Mediation in Practice,* HMSO, London.

Matthews, R (1988) *Informal Justice?*, Sage, London.

Merry, S (1989) Myth and Practice in the Mediation Process, in Wright, M and Galaway, B (eds) *Mediation and Criminal Justice*, Sage, London.

Messmer, H (1992) Communication in Decision-making about Diversion and Victim-offender Mediation, in Messmer, H and Otto, H-U (eds) *Restorative Justice on Trial*, Kluwer Academic Publishers, Dordrecht.

Millar, A R (1984) *The Experimental Introduction of Fines Enforcement Officers into Two Sheriff Courts*, Scottish Office, Central Research Unit, Edinburgh.

Moody, S and Tombs, J (1982) *Prosecution in the Public Interest*, Scottish Academic Press, Edinburgh.

National Audit Office (1989) *Prosecution of Crime in Scotland: Review of the Procurator Fiscal Service,* HMSO, London.

Nicholson, L (1990) *A Survey of Fine Defaulters in Scottish Courts,* Scottish Office, Central Research Unit, Edinburgh.

Nicholson, L (1992) *The Deferred Sentence in Scotland*, Scottish Office, Central Research Unit, Edinburgh.

Nicholson, L and Millar, A R (1989) *An Evaluation of a Fines Officer Scheme,* Scottish Office, Central Research Unit, Edinburgh.

Northmere, H (1988) Burglars and their Victims, *Mediation* vol 4, no 3, pp 5-7.

OPCS (1982) *General Household Survey 1981,* HMSO, London.

Parliamentary All-Party Penal Affairs Group (1984) *A New Deal for Victims,* PAPPAG, London.
Reeves, H (1989) The Victim Support Perspective, in Wright, M and Galaway, B (eds) *Mediation in the Criminal Justice System*, Sage, London.
Ruddick, R (1989) A Court Referral Scheme, in Wright, M and Galaway, B (eds) *Mediation in the Criminal Justice System*, Sage, London.
SACRO Reparation and Mediation Project (1989) *First Annual Report*, SACRO, Edinburgh.
SACRO Reparation and Mediation Project (1990) *Second Annual Report,* SACRO, Edinburgh.
Schwartz, I and Preiser, L (1992) Diversion and Juvenile Justice: Can We Ever Get it Right?, in Messmer, H and Otto, H-U (eds) *Restorative Justice on Trial,* Kluwer Academic Publishers, Dordrecht.
Scottish Home and Health Department (1989) Prison Statistics Scotland, *Statistical Bulletin*, vol 6, HMSO, Edinburgh.
Scottish Legal Aid Board (1990) *Scottish Legal Aid: Second Annual Report for the Year 1988-89*, HMSO, Edinburgh.
Shapland, J, Willmore, J and Duff, P (1985) *Victims in the Criminal Justice System,* Gower, Aldershot.
Smith, D and Blagg, H (1989b) The Cumbrian Reparation Scheme, *The British Journal of Social Work*, vol 19, pp 255-275.
Smith, D, Blagg, H and Derricourt, N (1989a) Mediation in the Shadow of the Law: The South Yorkshire Experience, in Mathews, R (ed) *Informal Justice?*, Sage, London.
Social Work Services Group (1988) Unpublished working paper on community service overheads, Scottish Office, Edinburgh.
Solicitor General (1988) Address to SACRO Conference, 7th October 1988, Edinburgh.
Stedward, G and Millar, A (1989) *Diversion from Prosecution, Volume 1, Diversion to Social Work,* Scottish Office, Central Research Unit, Edinburgh.
Tyler, T (1988) The Psychology of Disputants, *Mediation*, vol 4, no 3, pp 14-17.
Umbreit, M (1988) Mediation of Victim Offender Conflict, *Journal of Dispute Resolution*, vol 1988, pp 85-105.
Umbreit, M (1989a) Crime Victims Seeking Fairness, not Revenge: Towards Restorative Justice, *Federal Probation*, Sept 1989, pp 52-57.
Umbreit, M (1989b) Violent Offenders and their Victims, in Wright, M and Galaway, B (eds) *Mediation and Criminal Justice*, Sage, London.

Umbreit, M (1992) Mediating Victim-Offender Conflict: From Single-Site to Multi-Site Analysis in the U.S., in Messmer, H and Otto, H-U (eds) *Restorative Justice on Trial*, Kluwer Academic Publishers, Dordrecht.

Volpe, M (1989) The Police Role, in Wright, M and Galaway, B (eds) *Mediation and Criminal Justice*, Sage, London.

Warner, S (1992) Reparation, Mediation and Scottish Criminal Justice, in Messmer, H and Otto, H-U (eds) *Restorative Justice on Trial*, Kluwer Academic Press, Dordrecht.

Wright, M (1989) What the Public Wants, in Wright, M and Galaway, B (eds) *Mediation and Criminal Justice,* Sage, London.

Wright, M (1992) Victim/Offender Mediation as a Step Towards a Restorative System of Justice, in Messmer, H and Otto, H-U (eds) *Restorative Justice on Trial*, Kluwer Academic Publishers, Dordrecht.

Young, R (1986) *The Sandwell Mediation and Reparation Scheme*, West Midlands Probation Service, Birmingham.

Young, R (1989) Reparation as Mitigation, *Criminal Law Review,* pp 463-479.

Zehr, H (1985) *Retributive Justice, Restorative Justice,* US Office of Criminal Justice.

Zehr, H (1989) *Reparation: Where from Here?,* Forum for Initiatives in Reparation and Mediation, Beaconhurst.

Index

Index compiled by Ann Barham